THROUGH THE FIRE

THROUGH

SPIRITUAL

RESTORATION

THE FIRE

FOR ADULT VICTIMS OF CHILDHOOD SEXUAL ABUSE

by Rick Meyer

MINNEAPOLIS

Special thanks to Pamela Johnson for the prayers
of restoration found at the end of each chapter

THROUGH THE FIRE
Spiritual Restoration for Adult Victims of Childhood Sexual Abuse

Large-quantity purchases or custom editions of this book are available at
a discount from the publisher. For more information, contact the sales
department at Augsburg Fortress, Publishers, 1-800-328-4648, or write to:
Sales Director, Augsburg Fortress, Publishers, P. O. Box 1209, Minneapolis,
MN 55440-1209.

Scripture is taken from the *Holy Bible, New International Version* ®, copyright ©
1973, 1978, 1984 International Bible Society. Used by permission of Zondervan
Publishing House. All rights reserved.

ISBN 0-8066-5132-6

Chapter opener illustrations © Jonathan Rogers (www.artbyjonathan.com)

Cover design by Diana Running; cover photos © Photodisc/Getty Images
Book design by Michelle L. N. Cook

The paper used in this publication meets the minimum requirements of
American National Standard for Information Sciences—Permanence of
Paper for Printed Library Materials, ANSI Z329.48-1984. ® ™

Manufactured in the U.S.A.

09   08   07   06   05   1   2   3   4   5   6   7   8   9   10

"To those who have traveled so far,
and to those who are just beginning the journey . . .
through the fire"

CONTENTS

INTRODUCTION

Why I Wrote This Book

I wrote this book for those who have been sexually abused as children as well as for those who want to understand the abused. The subject is so painful that most of us, given the opportunity, would like to move quickly past it and on to something more comfortable. But sometimes, to really appreciate another person and his or her experiences, we have to be willing to venture close, to step alongside of that person and listen to the most horrible evils that this world can inflict.

In this book I contend that childhood sexual abuse is demonic, and that the only way a person so abused can experience peace and joy is through God's intervention. I also contend, however, that because God is often viewed as having failed to protect those who have been abused, they will have great difficulty accepting God's love until the cross of Jesus is understood as God's suffering of hell. Only a God who is familiar with such sufferings will be allowed to come close to one who has been sexually abused.

I invite you to join me on a journey toward understanding. Not a full experiential understanding, but a close enough look so that you feel a personal connection with the injured. If you have been a victim, then I want you to experience healing. If you know someone who is a victim, then I want you to become an advocate. To this end, this book is designed with a three-fold movement, from Pre-Death to Death, and then onto New Life. This is the movement of the healing process for the adult victim of childhood sexual abuse, and this will be the movement of the book as you read it.

Most importantly, I want you to see Jesus as an experienced, capable, compassionate companion for the journey. He has experienced a depth of trauma and abandonment that compares well with the suffering of the abused. The abuse that Jesus underwent makes him uniquely qualified to step alongside those who have been abused throughout all three phases of healing: Pre-Death, Death, and New Life.

"Fire" is one of the most frequently recurring images and feelings that I hear expressed by victims of childhood sexual abuse as they describe their struggles. "I feel like I'm trapped in a fire and there's no way out. I feel helpless to find relief." In fact, the sense of self has been so terribly shattered that the concept of "restoration" must become palpable, physical, and equally consuming if the survivor is to begin feeling the love and presence of God. The goal isn't to remove the heat, to stop the ability to feel. The goal is to take that which has been experienced as destructive and allow it to become purifying and strengthening to the soul, to calm the unbearable heat of the flames so that those flames become warm, soft embers that bring comfort instead of pain.

In this book I want to help victims and those who love them understand the journey through hell and the movement toward spiritual restoration. Through Roger's nightmares, Amy's thoughts of suicide, Sarah's detachment, and Debra's sabotaging of relationships, I want you to see more clearly the effects of sexual abuse. Through Amber's struggle with intimacy, David's sexual dysfunction, Jennifer's grieving process, and Teri's capacity for nurture, I want you to discover a common path to recovery. Ultimately, I want you to see that Jesus is an experienced guide who can and will assist in this journey toward health and wholeness. The bloodstained cross will be our emblem, our source of courage, and our comfort along the way. Spiritual restoration will be our ultimate goal.

How I Wrote This Book

I never expected to spend so much time working with victims of childhood sexual abuse. I wasn't prepared for the prevalence of this issue. The more people who shared their hurtful pasts with me, the more I learned how high the numbers actually are. Conservative estimates for girls ages fifteen and under suggest that one-in-four experience sexual abuse, while one-in-six boys ages fifteen and under are victims of sexual abuse. These numbers reflect my own practice. Consequently, in this book I highlight the stories of five women to every one man. The stories recounted here are composites of real-life stories. I have changed the names and details to protect individuals' privacy. Whether they are stories of women or men, the stories are compelling and real, and it is my hope that you cannot listen in without feeling both a deep sense of compassion and outrage.

Some of my personal questions about working with victims of sexual abuse revolved around the fact that I had never been so abused myself. Could I truly connect with victims of sexual abuse in a meaningful way? Would I have any credibility in their eyes? Was it possible to plunge into such depths of despair with another and live to tell about it? Was I in over my head? In the end I decided to become a companion and walk alongside people with the intention of seeing and feeling and learning from the experienced traveler. I also decided to keep the journey moving and not to get stuck in one place for too long. Hope requires forward motion. And spiritual restoration requires hope.

Without a doubt, my time spent in the depths of hell with adult survivors has been the most difficult and most rewarding work that I have ever experienced. I have learned more about the horrors of evil than I ever wanted to imagine. And I have seen the grace of God outpoured in ways beyond comprehension. Most importantly, I have seen the wounds of Jesus become a source of healing when no relief was in sight.

The theological distinction between God and Satan makes sense against the backdrop of abuse. This spiritual battle finds its greatest expression in the victim because the stakes are so high. The battle is for the soul. All of the therapeutic skill in the world, while important, is not enough. Maybe this is what Jesus had in mind when he said, "Some things can only be accomplished through prayer and fasting."

There are a number of good books available on the subject of recovery for adult victims of childhood sexual abuse, but only a few that connect the therapeutic aspects of healing to the spiritual restoration side of healing. As I recommended books to clients, I kept hearing a void in the area of practical, theological underpinnings. I felt the need to share stories in a way that would allow another person (victim or not) to "enter" the experiences of those who had been abused and to do this with the compassion of Christ.

I have learned from victims of sexual abuse that it is important to reflect on the suffering and death of Christ as a way to begin the healing process. Somehow the abused person needs to see how Jesus was rejected, tormented, and abandoned before they can allow God access to the heart they have learned to protect. Only a God who knows pain and death can provide healing and life. Only this kind of God really seems to matter in the end.

I have divided this book into three parts. Part 1 contains stories of Pre-Death and Death, part 2 looks at stories of New Life and part 3 shares some final thoughts on suffering. Jesus experienced Pre-Death as he spoke to his disciples and warned them of what he must endure. In some ways these Pre-Death discussions were probably as much for Jesus and his own sense of preparation as they were for the benefit of his disciples. Our Lord's anguish and questioning in the Garden of Gethsemane demonstrates the difference between talking about what needs to happen and actually going through with it. And so it is for the adult victim who also wants to enjoy healing and New Life. The Pre-Death and Death parts of the healing process are frightening beyond imagination. Even Jesus cried out from the cross, "My God, my God, why have you forsaken me?" (Matthew 27:46). Certainly there is no clearer definition of hell than total separation (or abandonment) from God. Who would willingly choose this path?

Jesus chose the path of suffering and death. And Jesus holds his nail-scarred hands out to those who desire to walk with him toward health and wholeness. His love is born out of this suffering and death, and he has the marks to prove it. Each chapter begins with a picture that sets the tone for what follows, including images of the Savior's nail-scarred hands. These images of our Lord are messages of hope, for these hands belong to one who is on the other side of suffering and death. These scars tell us who he is. These hands speak of New Life in him.

Not all of the images at the beginning of each chapter are those of our Lord. You will hopefully find your own hands here, your own life and journey. From the grasping of a tiny hand to the safe resting of a sleeping child to the holding of two hands clasped in friendship, I hope you will find yourself along the way. Each of these images created by Jonathan Rogers conveys a sensitivity that understands suffering and the need for a healing touch from God.

Now I invite you to journey with me through the fire toward spiritual restoration. Like the burnt forest on the cover of this book, my travels with victims of sexual abuse have shown me that the barrenness will give way to a new floor of green grass. The bloom of a flower on the forest floor will signal the beginning of New Life. My prayer is that you will come to see Jesus as your trusted companion along the way.

PART ONE

STORIES OF
PRE-DEATH
AND DEATH

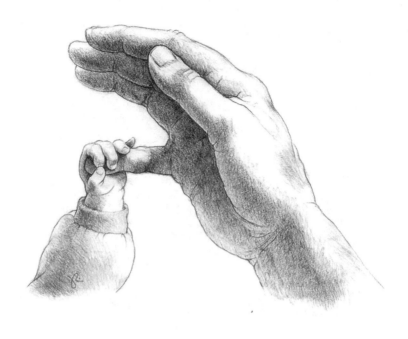

I remember when my children were small enough that they could only hold my pinky as we walked. I had never felt more important or needed, and all they could grasp was one small finger. And so it is in our relationship with God. God is so big, and we are so small. All that we can grasp is a fraction of who God is, and yet what comfort that small portion gives.

This child's hand represents the outrageous confidence that is required for an adult to trust another as she recovers from the trauma of childhood sexual abuse. This new hand is present to help and guide. The victim of sexual abuse must take hold and learn to trust again. This was Debra's journey.

CHAPTER ONE

SABOTAGING RELATIONSHIPS

Debra, age 32

Debra was a very capable and attractive young woman who had been married for seven years and had a three-year-old son. She came for counseling because she was beginning to experience a pervasive depression and was seriously questioning her commitment to her marriage. She felt detached from her husband, and she had been withdrawing from sex. In fact, she couldn't remember a time when she actually enjoyed sex. Before giving up on the marriage completely, however, she had decided to seek help.

As we reviewed Debra's family history, I discovered that her parents had divorced when she was seven. At this time she went to live with her mother and stepfather. For a period of five years, from age seven to twelve, Debra was sexually abused by her stepfather with her mother's full knowledge and consent. In addition, her mother sexually abused Debra's younger brother. As Debra put it, they all piled into one bed and the feeding frenzy began.

Debra recalls how she experienced a confusing mixture of feelings as a child. On the one hand, she felt ashamed and disgusted by her stepfather's actions. On the other hand, she sometimes felt proud that she was beginning to develop physically and could be attractive to a man. More often than not, she simply felt helpless and afraid in the face of her mother's betrayal. Her mother and stepfather warned her not to tell anyone about the sexual activities. They threatened to send her brother away if she told anyone, so she kept it to herself.

Fortunately an extended family member learned about the sexual abuse and contacted Debra's father who immediately took action to secure her safety and that of her brother. He was awarded full custody while the mother could only attend supervised visits. Debra never heard from her mother again accept for a card one Christmas. As far as Debra was concerned, this was one card (or contact) too many. She didn't want anything to do with her mother ever again.

Debra experienced a very turbulent adolescence. She angered easily, left home for days at a time without telling anyone where she was, and began using marijuana and alcohol at an early age. Her father and stepmother attended family counseling hoping that they could resolve their problems, but Debra simply folded her arms, looked away, and told her family and the counselor to go to hell. She didn't care about anything or anyone. She was going to do whatever she wanted whenever, and anyone who tried to get in her way was looking for a fight. Needless to say, this family suffered greatly.

Debra was out of control, but also very intelligent. She graduated from high school and went on to college where she obtained a bachelor's degree in finance. It was during her college years that Debra began to seriously explore her spirituality for the first time. Although, she didn't think of herself as religious and organized religion turned her off, she was beginning to search and ask the big questions of life.

Debra met some girls who seemed to genuinely care about her and wanted her to attend a Bible study with them. The last time Debra had attended any kind of church service had been with her grandmother when she was thirteen. All she could remember from that experience was how she sat in the pew wondering how a God who was supposed to be so powerful and loving could have let her suffer so badly. God didn't seem very relevant or friendly. But she decided to attend the Bible study with her friends and did so several times.

Debra enjoyed the Bible study, the conversations about faith, and the freedom to ask searching questions about God. However, Debra was easily overwhelmed by any type of emotional closeness. For example, once the campus pastor innocently put his hand on her shoulder and Debra just froze up. She didn't let on how uncomfortable she felt, but the fear was completely debilitating. People in the group liked Debra and wanted to get closer to her. At first she seemed to welcome this interest, but then one day out of nowhere she severed her relationship with the group and never went back.

Debra had a history of starting to get close to people (something she very much desired and needed) only to sever the relationships abruptly because of the feeling of overwhelming fear. Now Debra was beginning to repeat this pattern in her relationship with her husband and, with her three-year-old son in mind, she was afraid of doing irreparable damage to the people she cared about most.

Early in our counseling relationship Debra told me that she wanted to feel closer to God and that she needed to stop sabotaging her marriage due to her emotional responses to various triggers (sights, sounds, and other sensory experiences that reminded her of the childhood sexual abuse). We needed to find a way to integrate Debra's relationship with God, her past abuse, and the present triggers.

One of the best ways that I have found to accomplish this integration is through letter-writing. I asked Debra to imagine that her stepfather, the abuser, had died and that God had come to her with a request that she write a letter to her stepfather expressing how she feels about him. Debra was reluctant to participate until I explained that she would not actually send the letter to her stepfather.

This seemed to ease her fears. The suggestion that God was giving her permission and inviting her to express her emotions gave Debra a sense of peace about the assignment. Her letter was powerful.

Dear Charles,

I am glad you have died. You can never molest and damage any more children; the world is a better place now that you are gone. I am deeply relieved knowing no one else will be tortured by your evil desires.

I do not remember anything about you that wasn't evil. To me you are the epitome of evil and represent the devil himself. Memories of you will haunt me forever. I am sorry my Christianity isn't strong enough to grant you forgiveness. I doubt I ever will.

You had no right to steal my innocence and leave me forever scared. Your "need" and desire for constant unnatural sexual satisfaction is appalling and sickening. I cannot nor will I ever understand your attraction to an eight-year-old girl (nor a five-year-old boy and his mother). All I can fathom is that something was severely wrong with you and I do not care what caused it. There is no excuse or justification. I do not believe you feel any remorse or that you care.

I am constantly reminded of the pain caused by your sinful desires. I am still battling with the ability to watch most movies, hear jokes, or deal with any other little incident of a sexual nature without being bothered. This is even affecting my marriage and I hate you for that. Your minutes of gratification have become a lifetime of misery for me. Will I be able to live life without being affected by your sin?

God has helped me begin to live a more normal
life. I pray God will continue to guide me so that I
can reach a point of handling daily life without seeing
the evilness everywhere. I pray that some day I will be
strong enough to focus on using my life to serve God,
instead of focusing on just getting through the day.

Debra

This letter gave Debra the opportunity to confront her abuser without doing so directly. She also had the chance to begin more fully exploring the resources of her Christian faith as an aid in her search for increased health and wholeness. And this exercise helped Debra give voice to the fact that something that happened so many years ago could have such a profound affect in the present.

Debra's letter, in addition to helping her confront her personal pain, is a poignant example of the basic elements that I encounter whenever I work with someone who has been sexually abused as a child. The elements along with explanations are as follows:

1) Relief at the death of the perpetrator so that he or she can no longer hurt another child

A frequent desire expressed by the victim is for the perpetrator to die. With the abuser's death, the victim hopes to feel less afraid and, as Debra pointed out, the person won't be able to hurt anyone else.

2) The perpetrator is viewed as the personification of evil ("the devil himself")

This view of the perpetrator as "devil-like" seems to be an important part of the healing process for the victim.

Even though God may have allowed this horrible crime to occur, there must be a way to name the evil as distinctly separate from God.

3) A personal feeling that one's Christian faith is too weak to deal adequately with the abuse

Recovery from childhood sexual abuse is a profoundly spiritual experience. I have yet to speak with a victim for whom this is not the case. Issues such as anger and disappointment with God, the concepts of guilt and shame, as well as forgiveness for self and others all require special attention.

4) Bewilderment over how anyone could commit such a heinous crime

This feeling of bewilderment or confusion is actually a hopeful sign. The depth of disgust that resides in the victim toward the abuser and his or her actions is a significant indicator of the depth of love that the abused has for life as a good gift in and of itself. This is important in light of the fact that victims generally have a difficult time seeing the beautiful side of life.

5) A constant battle with normal, everyday experiences that act as triggers for the abuse

Basic sensory experiences such as sights, sounds, and smells can act as triggers to remind the individual of the past abuse. In this way what occurred in the past actually becomes re-experienced in the present.

6) The residual affect of the past abuse on current relationships, such as a marriage

Even good emotional experiences, such as an affectionate look from a husband or wife, or a particular tender touch can elicit a reactive response based upon past abusive experiences. Such reactions can play havoc on important and otherwise healthy relationships as the victim seeks to reestablish a feeling of safety.

7) A tendency to overemphasize the evilness in the world to the exclusion of anything good

A black-or-white, all-or-nothing approach to belief systems and relationships is a hallmark of the abused as a way to establish a sense of security. Also, the victim tends to see the glass as half empty and draining fast.

8) A desire to not merely survive, but to thrive

The victim doesn't want to be a "victim" any longer. He or she wants the old self to be renewed in such a way that the goodness and beauty of life become the predominant images and experience.

These eight elements will be woven throughout the stories of the people in this book. Some elements may be more apparent in one person than another. Together, though, these elements help to form the common pathway for the healing and wholeness that all of the victims in this book desire.

Debra frequently complained of feeling an overall lack of energy. Her efforts to just make it through a day left her exhausted and despairing. Everywhere she turned in our sexualized culture there were reminders of how women are objectified and degraded. As she said, "Some days I don't want to go outside or turn on a TV or radio. I just want to go someplace where I don't feel bombarded with images and messages of irresponsible sex."

As Debra and I talked, we shifted our attention to the cross of Christ. We talked about how Jesus was beaten and spat upon, how the crown of thorns was shoved on his head, and how the skin on his back and sides was lashed and torn. As he hung upon the cross, the nails piercing his hands and feet, Jesus said, "I am thirsty" (John 19:28). This is the Son of God who created the oceans. This is the one who turned water into wine. And this is the same one who mixed his saliva with dirt to place upon a blind man's eyes and restore his sight. Now he thirsts? How simple. How ordinary. And yet in the midst of great suffering it is the sop of a vinegar-drenched sponge that brought him comfort.

Debra connected with the image of Jesus as he asked for something to drink. She understood how important it was to receive a little help, a little hope, some small bit of comfort in the midst of her hell. Tears began to well up in her eyes, then large drops fell to her lap. "Maybe God understands my misery better than I had imagined," she said.

The discussion about Jesus's suffering on the cross was an important point of connection for Debra in her faith journey.

Prayer

Dearest Jesus,
You understand my misery better than I imagined.
Thank you for staying with me.
Help me to stop sabotaging my relationships.
Heal my fear.
Restore my spirit.
Amen.

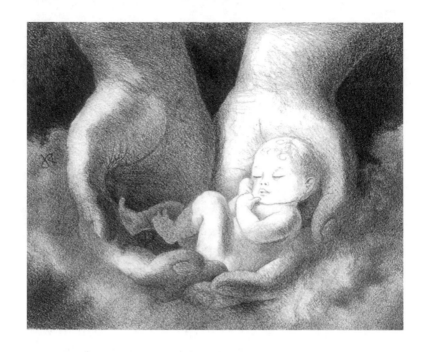

This is the image of a precious child too young to notice its need for the hands that hold it. This is a picture of assurance for one who feels the constant battle of mind and heart. Even the large hands are overlapping as if to say, "You can count on me."

For Jessica, thoughts and emotions race in her mind while diametrically opposed ideas compete for space and battle for dominion. Happy one minute, sad the next. Anguish in one part of her heart, and comfort in another. How confusing it all seems. Jessica simply needs to feel the security of God's embrace.

CHAPTER TWO

CONFLICTING THOUGHTS AND EMOTIONS

Jessica, age 23

Jessica was a first-year graduate student studying business law when she came to me complaining of sleeplessness and panic attacks. This wasn't the first time that Jessica had experienced these symptoms, but lately they had increased in frequency, intensity, and duration. She had a physical examination, and her general practitioner suggested that she might benefit from counseling.

Jessica grew up on a rural, mid-western farm together with two younger sisters. All three of the girls had been molested by their father during their early adolescence. He started with Jessica, the oldest, and then worked his way down the line as each girl progressed in age.

The father would come into the girls' room at night and lie in bed with one of them. The other two would either be asleep or acting as though they were asleep so as not to let on that they knew what was happening. The girls never discussed with one another what had happened until the third and youngest sister became a regular target. It was around this time that the father's deeds were exposed, and the girls were split up and sent to live with different relatives while their mother and father remained on the farm together.

Jessica had never before discussed the molestation by her father in depth until we began to meet on a weekly basis. She had started to read the novel, *A Thousand Acres*, about three sisters who grew up on a farm where each had been sexually abused by their father. It was while reading this book, a recommended reading from one of her undergraduate classes, that Jessica began to experience her greatest problems with sleeplessness and anxiety. The story of the three sisters simply hit too close to home. In many ways this was her story, and she wanted to confront her demons before they destroyed her self-worth completely.

One of the recurring themes in Jessica's life was her poor choice of boyfriends. She would date guys who took advantage of her sexually. Afterward, these men would end their relationship with Jessica until they wanted sex with her again. Then they would turn on the charm and Jessica would fall for them all over again. In Jessica's mind, sex was equated with love. The only way she knew how to feel close to a man was through sexual expression. She was a bright and intelligent woman, however, in this area, Jessica was terribly misguided. She was setting herself up for constant hurt and rejection.

Confused thoughts and emotions are a hallmark of those who have been sexually abused. At an early and formative age, a trusted and respected person violated the emotional and physical boundaries of a child leaving him or her feeling conflicted about how to separate good from bad, right from wrong, and respect from disrespect. The implicit message to the child is, "I know what's best for you, and you can trust me. Even though this sexual abuse may feel bad or wrong, it is actually good and right. You just need to find a way to accept it. Otherwise, you will drive yourself insane since you're not big enough or strong enough to change your situation. Simply tell yourself over and over again that everything will be all right so that you can endure this. In fact, since everyone has a sex drive, which is natural and normal, you might even like some of what you feel. Whatever you do, don't fight it."

It's no wonder that a victim of sexual abuse carries a warped sense of boundary formation into young adulthood. To a victim of sexual abuse one of two extremes seems to be the only option. Either she allows herself to be taken advantage of sexually or she detaches sexually altogether. That place "in the middle" between extremes is unimaginable and therefore unattainable.

As is often my practice with those who have been sexually abused, I invited Jessica to keep track of her dreams. The first dream she recorded was an account of her life at home with her parents and two sisters:

> *My youngest sister got up in the middle of the night and broke the fish tank that stood in the hallway outside the bedrooms. The fish died and water went everywhere. The strange part of the dream is that the water kept rising and rising until it was up to our necks. Everyone had to tread water until we could make it outside the house to safety. The house was entirely destroyed. Then I woke up.*

I asked Jessica what the elements of the dream connected to in her life. She explained that the fish tank outside the bedroom represented something that was supposed to be taken care of and protected like the family secret of abuse. Once the silence (fish tank) was broken, the repercussions were overwhelming like a flood. The home was destroyed, and the children could never return again.

Somehow by seeing the family secret as an entity unto itself, Jessica was better able to separate herself from the abuse and name it for the evil that it was without indicting herself in any way. She began to see her childhood innocence behind the bedroom doors. She began to love the little girl whom she found there tucked quietly in her bed.

The next dream that Jessica recorded included just her and her two sisters driving in a car together:

I was behind the wheel and my sisters were both passengers in the front seat with me, the youngest in the middle. The three of us drove for a long period of time attempting to get somewhere, but we kept driving around in circles. Finally we started down a hill, one that we had driven many times before. However, this time the brakes didn't work and we were headed for a wall. At the last minute, my youngest sister grabbed the steering wheel and the car pulled to the side away from the wall. Then I woke up.

"What does all of this mean?" I asked. Jessica knew in an instant that the car driving in circles represented the abuse and the loss of brakes stood for a loss of control. The youngest sister grabbing the wheel represented the exposure of the abuse and their subsequent removal from home. Then Jessica said, "I still don't know where I'm going in life, but at least I didn't hit the wall. In other words, I'm still alive, not happy, but alive. I just don't understand why I was unable to turn the steering wheel or get out of the abusive situation myself. I always knew that what my father was doing was wrong, but somehow I was more afraid of what would happen if I told than I was afraid of what he was doing."

Parts Language and Conflicted Emotions

Across time I introduced the concept of "parts" language into our discussion. As I explained to Jessica, we tend to naturally think and talk about ourselves in terms of a variety of parts. For example, when someone asks our opinion about something such as the prospect of moving to a new city, we might say, "Part of me feels excited and part of me feels afraid. On the other hand, part of me feels at peace about the decision." All three of these emotions are real and present in our experience at one and the same time. Somehow we can have more than one thought, feeling, or emotion standing side-by-side in a given instance. I often find this "part's language" concept helpful in the process of integrating the conflicting thoughts and feelings experienced by one who has been sexually abused.

One of the greatest frustrations for the survivor of sexual abuse seems to be the experience of multiple thoughts and feelings occurring at the same time. Survivors will simultaneously feel hatred and love, discomfort and pleasure, joy and sorrow, fear and reassurance—each contrasting pair leaves the individual feeling confused and looking for a way to reconcile the apparent disparity. Most often a survivor will chose one extreme or the other.

All of this frustration can be traced back to the confusion that existed as a child; the abused may have felt loyalty and love toward the abuser, and at the same time disgust and hatred. Often the only way to endure what was happening at the time was to somehow imagine that certain thoughts or feelings were either unreliable or dangerous. The abused often learns to turn the most negative thoughts and feelings inward, suggesting that there must be something wrong with her- or himself. In other words, negative thoughts and emotions such as hatred, disgust, and shame are not seen as qualities that exist outside of the person her- or himself.

Jessica was very receptive to the idea of looking at people in the Bible who had multiple, even diametrically opposed feelings at the same time. We talked about the man who asked Jesus to heal his son who was near death. Jesus turned to the man and said, "Everything is possible for him who believes." The man replied, "I do believe; help me overcome my unbelief!" (Mark 9:23-24). This man had belief, faith, and trust, yet at the very same time he felt doubt, despair, fear, and even unbelief. This isn't something to feel ashamed of. Rather, this is a real-life example for all of us.

Perhaps the most important example of a biblical person struggling with conflicting thoughts and emotions is found in Jesus. Several times during his earthly ministry Jesus tried to prepare his disciples for the fact that he would have to suffer and die, but on the third day after his death he would rise from the dead. He seemed to speak these words almost matter-of-factly. This is what will happen, he said, so don't be surprised. When the hour finally came, however, we find Jesus in the Garden of Gethsemane praying to the Father in heaven, saying, "If it would be possible [if there is any other way to accomplish what you want], please remove this cup of judgment [this suffering and death] from me." And he didn't stop at just one prayer. No, he prayed three times. Finally, in the face of his Father's silence, Jesus resigns himself to the Father's will. In other words, even though Jesus knew ahead of time what his mission would entail (namely, suffering, and death) he still felt conflicted in his spirit. He must have been terror stricken at the prospect of such a horrifying and shameful death. And yet he chose this most difficult way. As a result, we know we have a Lord who understands our afflictions and sorrows and fears. Indeed, Jesus must love us very much!

Jessica discovered a fellow traveler in the person of Jesus, one familiar with conflicted thoughts and feelings like herself. The greatest depths of agony and abuse are full of disparity and confusion. Nothing seems to make sense when you're in pain. It's hard to think clearly. How wonderful it was for Jessica to see that Jesus was comforted by the knowledge that His Father was with him even in his darkest hours. Jesus didn't fully experience this comfort until he let go of life on the cross. Jessica was also learning to let go of what she could not control and trust God to keep her safely in the palm of his hand.

Prayer

Dearest Jesus,
I have such conflicted thoughts and emotions.
You have traveled the same path.
Thank you for showing me that it is human to feel two
*   things at once.*
Thank you for your humanness.
Help me accept mine.
Help me rest in your safety and compassion.
Amen.

Is it possible that our Lord's compassion for us is equal to or greater than the suffering he experienced upon the cross? How utterly alone he must have felt as others looked on. Surely this great act was intended to get our attention, to help us see what is most important in life.

When Jesus hung upon the cross, he chose his words carefully. These were his last words before his death, and as such, they betrayed the greatest burdens of his heart. Along with a word of forgiveness, Jesus urged his disciples to care for one another as family. In the following story, Amy learns how fear leads to panic and rage as well as the value of friendship and the healing power of presence.

CHAPTER THREE

FEAR THAT LEADS
TO PANIC AND RAGE

Swimming Laps and Healing Fears
(Our Bodies Remember)

I remember the first time that I began to more fully understand the trigger response for panic in those who have been sexually abused. I was swimming laps for exercise at the local YMCA. Down and back was one lap. Then down and back again for two laps. Then down and . . . panic . . . gasping for air and kicking hard to make it to the end. I stopped and focused on slowing my breathing. "What was that?" I said to myself. I had felt a wave of fear come over me during the swim. After I settled down, I tried to continue. Down and back for another lap. Then down and . . . a sudden fear of drowning! "This is crazy," I thought. But then I remembered.

When I was eight-years-old, an older girl held me underwater at the local pool. I remember fighting to get free and losing energy until finally she let go of me. I made it to the side of the pool panicking and gasping for air. I never felt quite the same about water after that incident. I was always a little abnormally afraid. And now, in the pool thirty years later, I was experiencing the same panic all over again. The interesting thing was that my body remembered before I could actually recall the incident that occurred at age eight.

In Babette Rothschild's book, *The Body Remembers,* she discusses somatic memory (soma means "body") in relation to the experience of trauma, whether it be the more severe types as found in wartime Post-traumatic Stress Disorder and Childhood Sexual Abuse, or something more mild like my swimming incident. Rothschild explains that the body-mind connection is such that the body may respond to a trigger event (for me this was the act of swimming laps) with the same emotional and physical/muscular reflexes as if the original event was occurring all over again. And this body response can occur without any clear mental recollections of the original event.

Regarding the Somatic Nervous System (SomNS), Rothschild explains: "State-dependent recall can sometimes be triggered through the SomNS by inadvertently (or purposely) assuming a posture inherent in a traumatic situation. When used purposefully, it can aid the possibility of memory recall and/or reestablishment of behavioral resources. Reconstructing the movements involved in a fall or a car accident can often accomplish this. However, when state-dependent recall hits unexpectedly, it can cause chaos."

> *A mid-thirties woman sought therapy for panic that developed while making love with her husband. Her arm had accidentally gotten caught under her in an awkward position, firing off memories of a rape she thought she had long put behind her. The rapist had pinned the same arm under her in the same position.*

In my case, I decided to continue swimming laps with the hope that eventually I would have enough positive experiences to help counter the negative one. It took about a year of swimming laps three times a week before I recognized a decrease in my feelings of panic. Today I can say that it has been a good two years since feeling that way. On some level I know that those feelings of panic could return. However the idea of panic rarely enters my conscious thoughts and doesn't seem to keep me from enjoying a good swim.

What about the person who has suffered childhood sexual abuse? What is the prognosis for recovery for someone so traumatized? Those who work with victims of abuse usually see a range of symptoms depending upon the age of the child at the time of the abuse, the severity and duration of the abuse, and the level of support within the family following the revelation of abuse. However, therapists commonly observe that each individual is unique and that what may have more lasting effects for one person may not have the same effects on another person who experiences the same level of abuse. Without exception, the resultant effects of abuse are profound for anyone having experienced sexual abuse regardless of age, severity, and duration.

Obviously, my swimming experience is only illustrative of the body-memory effects of traumatic events. There is no way to really compare this with the experience of childhood sexual abuse. There is a hopeful parallel, though, in that one who has experienced abuse can over time enjoy the restoration and healing of the fragmented self through desensitization training and regular trust-building exercises. And in my experience, the realization that God, through Jesus, experientially understands suffering and is key to attaining spiritual wholeness.

Amy, age 39

Amy was a medical researcher, in her second marriage, and did not have any children nor did she want any children. She came to me for counseling because of some recent anxiety attacks and a growing fear that her husband would one day leave her. I met with the couple together and individually in an attempt to assess the nature of Amy's concerns.

Amy's husband, Douglas, was a mild mannered, even passive, individual. Like Amy, he worked in the field of medical research and, also like Amy, worked very long hours. He had been previously married and had a daughter by that marriage who lived with her mother. Douglas complained that Amy had periodic outbursts, what could only be described as rage. And, as Douglas said, "The punishment didn't fit the crime." Some small, insignificant thing would act as a trigger and Amy would yell uncontrollably. Over the past several months this behavior had become more frequent and intense.

Douglas knew that Amy had been sexually abused as a child, but he didn't understand how something that happened so long ago could be felt so intensely today. Why, he wondered, was he the frequent target of her anger? He had begun spending more time at work, they slept in separate beds, and the "d" word had even been brought up. Neither one wanted a divorce, partly because they shared a commitment to the marriage and partly because their religious upbringing taught them that divorce was wrong. But neither one wanted to go on living together in the same way. Something needed to change.

I'm always thankful whenever I see a faith-based commitment to the institution of marriage. Many marriages simply wouldn't last long enough to discover the gift that has been given if not for the underpinnings of faith. Amy and Douglas were certainly no different in this regard. By the time they came to see me they didn't really like each other and were feeling they had made a big mistake by marrying. I knew that we would have to pay close attention to the marriage along with Amy's childhood abuse if this couple was going to make it.

Unfortunately, the couple didn't make it. Douglas appeared beaten down and depressed. He lost all hope for the survival of his marriage to Amy and he became involved emotionally with another woman at work. Amy filed for divorce, and I never saw Douglas again. However, Amy and I continued to meet on a weekly basis for a year as she desired to address the affects of her childhood abuse.

Amy had been brutally and sexually abused by a stepfather from the age of seven to fifteen. She had four other brothers and sisters, all of whom were abused together and made to abuse one another. The stepfather threatened to kill their mother if they told of his activities and so they remained silent to protect her. Amy, the oldest, was recruited early on to be a surrogate mother to her siblings and she always felt ashamed that she was unable to protect them from the stepfather. The only way she learned to give her siblings and herself some relief (since the stepfather became physically abusive if the children were uncooperative) was to offer herself sexually to the stepfather and make sure that she satisfied him so that he wouldn't have reason to seek attention from the other children. Fortunately, an alert teacher at school picked up on some signs of abuse in one of Amy's younger brothers and Child Protection Services was called in to investigate. The stepfather was charged and sent to prison for twenty years.

Amy's stepfather has now been released. Although she believes that he lives several states away, Amy frequently fears that he will come and brutalize her again. She describes feeling as though he will reach out from underneath her car and grab her as she starts to climb in. During these moments her heart races, she feels light-headed, and she sweats profusely. The anxiety can be overwhelming and debilitating to the point that she needs to take medicine and go home to sleep for the rest of the day. Lately, the experience of panic has been more frequent and severe.

I asked Amy to pay close attention to her dreams, keeping a pen and paper next to her bed to record what she could remember upon waking. She eventually reported a recurring image, a nightmare. Amy saw herself bowing before a huge flame of fire, and she was covered in blood. She felt completely degraded and worthless, as though she was dying an infinite death. She never felt relief. The torment was unending. Amy asked if I had ever known anyone else who felt this way. I shared with her a prayer that another person had written during his darkest time of life:

> *O Lord, the God who saves me,*
> *day and night I cry out before you.*
> *May my prayer come before you;*
> *turn your ear to my cry.*
>
> *You have put me in the lowest pit,*
> *in the darkest depths.*
> *Your wrath lies heavily upon me;*
> *you have overwhelmed me with all*
> *your waves.*
> *You have taken from me my closest*
> *friends*
> *and have made me repulsive to them.*
> *I am confined and cannot escape;*
> *my eyes are dim with grief.*
>
> *But I cry to you for help, O Lord;*
> *in the morning my prayer comes*
> *before you.*

Why, O Lord, do you reject me
  and hide your face from me?
From my youth I have been afflicted
and close to death;
  I have suffered your terrors and am
in despair.
Your wrath has swept over me;
  your terrors have destroyed me.
All day long they surround me like a
flood;
  they have completely engulfed me.
You have taken my companions and
loved ones from me;
  the darkness is my closest friend.

This prayer is actually a portion of Psalm 88 and just one of the many personal laments that occur in the Bible. Personally, I have found the inclusion of such prayers in the Bible to be very encouraging since the people crying out to God are doing so in faith. These laments show that despair and suffering, even contempt for the Lord are all part of the faith journey that we experience in our relationship with God. It is as though God, through the Scriptures, is giving us permission, even inviting us to pour out our true feelings . . . and saying that God is big enough to take our grief, our anger, our pain.

Like the psalmist, Amy felt cut off from God, rejected and abandoned. She frequently experienced such engulfing shame that she saw herself as repulsive to others. She exclaimed, "How could anyone accept and love someone like me who has been so damaged? Why would anyone want to embrace me when I fill the air with the stench of human waste?" Amy connected with the psalmist's experience of feeling flooded by God's wrath and judgment. And the feeling of loneliness was simply unbearable. She said, "I know what the psalmist means when he says that the darkness is his closest friend."

Distinguishing between Guilt and Shame

As I often find with those who have been sexually abused, it was necessary to help Amy make a distinction between guilt and shame. I explained that guilt is when you feel good or bad about something that you have done or not done, while shame is feeling bad about who you are as a person. God never intended for us to feel shame. Unfortunately the literature on child abuse is replete with confusion between these two concepts of guilt and shame. Either guilt is downplayed as unhealthy because it has been equated with shame, or one might find a distinction between mild and severe forms of shame. In this instance, the Christian tradition with its distinction between guilt and shame is most helpful.

By embracing guilt as an important and healthy experience, we legitimize the victim's moral sense of disgust toward the perpetrator and abuse. The shame that the abused feels is so overwhelming that a clear image of right and wrong (or guilt) will be necessary if he or she can ever hope to keep from feeling as though the abuse was a deserved form of God's wrath.

As a by-product of the intense feeling of shame, a victim will often isolate herself from others due to a general feeling of unworthiness. This isolation, then, tends to feed into a cycle of depression which itself leads the person to feel even worse. In this regard, one of the most critical parts of the healing process includes helping the person to reengage, attach, and invest in relationships with others. For Amy, it was important for her to see Jesus as encouraging these relationships with other people.

Building a Community of Support

When Jesus hung upon the cross, having been brutalized and degraded, abandoned and alone, he looked with compassion upon those who stood nearby. In particular, he turned to his mother who was standing beside the disciple John and he said, "Behold [look and see] your son. Behold [look and see] your mother." In other words, Jesus was saying to them, "Take care of one another. Support and encourage one another as family. Don't be alone in your sorrow. You need each other."

Numerous studies have been conducted that underscore the fact that people who have a strong support system will become healthier faster than those without such support. This shouldn't come as a surprise to us since we are all born social creatures. Dependency on others is a part of our nature, whether we want to admit it or not. Jesus had his alone time, but always as an adjunct to his time with others—not the other way around. And what a great blessing it is when a person can enter a faith community where both support and eternal purposes are brought together in one place.

Amy was learning about the importance of community in her life. She began participating in a support group with four other women who had been sexually abused. She also started attending a Bible study with an older woman who Amy described as a "mentor." She was learning the importance of not being alone.

Prayer

Dearest Jesus,
The darkness is my closest friend.
I sometimes panic and do not know why.
I am afraid of my rage.
I give my panic and my rage to you.
Stay present. Stay near.
Thank you for the people you send to me.
I know that I am not alone.
Amen.

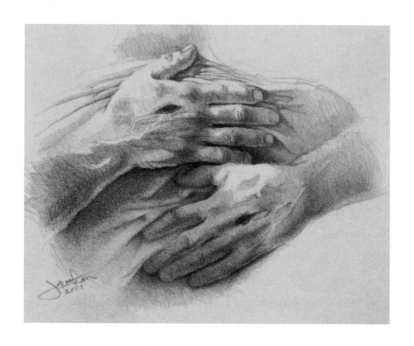

Henri Nouwen wrote a book called The Wounded Healer *in which he talks about how one who has been deeply hurt is often in the best position to understand the hurts of another. Jesus would often steal away in the middle of the night and sit in his father's presence. And always, in humility, he would listen to his father's voice. This was a place of shelter and comfort. This was a place of safety. From this place Jesus could emerge restored and ready to restore another.*

Sarah often felt separated from others by her experiences. The separation was felt internally, but also had external marks as well. When she emerged from her quiet place, though, she was not afraid to enter the darkness of another. And through Sarah, God offered shelter and comfort and safety to those in need.

CHAPTER FOUR

DISSOCIATION AND THE EMOTIONAL SELF

Sarah, age 42

Sarah was a divorced mother of two who was referred to me by her pastor because, as he explained it, "Sarah thinks everyone wants to have sex with her." Sarah didn't deny this. She really did think that most men only wanted this one thing from her. Lately, though, Sarah had begun to discuss openly at church her sexualized interpretations of Scripture, and others were growing increasingly uncomfortable around her. For example, in a woman's small group Bible study, Sarah expressed that she believed Psalm 23 was an attempt by God to place women under man's sexual domination. As she explained, "What else can God mean when he says, "Your *rod* and your staff, they comfort me?" Needless to say, her interpretation of Scripture caught everyone's attention.

It came as no surprise that Sarah was sexually abused as a child. From the age of eight until age thirteen, Sarah's father threw parties and scheduled times for Sarah to meet with different business associates for sexual activity. When Sarah was three her mother committed suicide by pouring gasoline over herself and setting herself on fire. Consequently, Sarah had no one else to turn to accept her father, and so she attempted to make the best of a very bad situation.

My insides hurt as I listened to Sarah's story. I'm sure she could see the pain on my face. And I couldn't help but think of my own two daughters. How unthinkable it would be for someone (especially a father) to treat his children this way. I knew that most childhood sexual abuse is committed by a family member or friend of the family. But other predators do exist, and they tend to be repeat offenders. I decided to check the Internet for information on convicted abusers in my own neighborhood. The world began to feel a little less safe that day.

As Sarah discussed her mother's death and the sexual abuse, she did so in a way that seemed devoid of emotion. She spoke matter-of-factly, saying, "It happened. So what can I do about it now? I have to move on with life." Sometimes Sarah would talk about feeling as though a part of her was missing. "I don't know what it is, but I just don't seem to respond to situations normally. Others get excited when they hear good news, or sad when they hear bad news. I, on the other hand, just listen without any spontaneous emotion at all. It's as though my emotional response system is shut down. It can even be a little embarrassing at times so I try to fake an appropriate response. It helps if there are others around whom I can cue off of." Certainly Sarah needed to make a healthy distinction between the past abuse and the present feelings of victimization; however, the lack of appropriate emotion—"a part missing"—was a reason for concern.

Whenever her father threw his parties, Sarah would try to hide in the bathroom by curling up in a ball behind the sink. Of course, her father always found her and brought her to the next man who was waiting for her in the bedroom. Sarah just stared far away during the sexual episodes, even felt detached to the point of leaving her body. "I would just go away somewhere in my mind for a while until the man was finished. Time seemed to stand still and I would think of Mary, the mother of Jesus. I always wanted to be like Mary. So pure and innocent. So loved by God."

Dissociation and Its Effects

Dissociation, or splitting, is the word used to describe the experience of a person who talks about a difficult, painful subject without the appropriate accompanying emotions. In Sarah's case, she would discuss her mother's death and her childhood abuse without so much as a twinge of feeling. It was as though all painful emotions were dissociated or split-off from the topic at hand ("I would just go away somewhere in my mind for a while until the man was finished"). And, as I came to learn over time, such a division or compartmentalization is common for victims of childhood sexual abuse.

Sarah was an emergency room nurse, which is a high stress profession. When she talked about her work she seemed to come alive with a certain intensity in her eyes. In many ways I had the impression that it was during her work that Sarah felt most alive, most fully present with herself. This impression fit with everything that I knew about those who have been sexually abused as children. In fact, one of my colleagues conducted a survey which indicated that a very high percentage, up to forty-six percent in some cases, of those in medical emergency professions have experienced significant childhood trauma. It's as though these individuals somehow feel most at ease and focused during a crisis.

Like Sarah, most of the people I see who have been sexually abused as children grow up to be intelligent, competent, overachievers. They may not experience a whole lot of success in their primary relationships. However, they certainly demonstrate a high level of personal ability and discipline. And when it comes to looking for someone who is thorough and a take-charge person, I've learned to look no farther than to a person who has experienced childhood sexual abuse. It's as though that person has made up her or his mind that the best way to succeed (or survive) in this world is to be in absolute control.

I guess it shouldn't come as a surprise that many adult survivors have become very successful in their chosen fields. For example, Oprah Winfrey (television and movie celebrity), Maya Angelou (author), Peter Lawford (actor), Kelly McGillis (actress), Fran Drescher (actress), Marilyn Van Derbur Atler (Miss America, 1958), LeToya Jackson (entertainer), Roseanne Barr (comedian), Liberace (musician), Marie Osmond (entertainer), Ann Sexton (writer), Carl Jung (psychologist, philosopher, and writer), Richard Pryor (entertainer), Erroll Flynn (actor), and Natalie Cole (entertainer) have all been public about their sexual abuse.

These are just a few recognizable names, noteworthy because of their public roles. I don't think anyone would deny that each one of these people has distinguished him- or herself with an unrelenting determination. Each one is a fairly intense individual known for being personally demanding. One should not imagine that a person who has been sexually abused will be huddled up in some corner afraid to pursue any goals. On the contrary, these are some of the most capable people I have ever known. These are also people who have been hurt more deeply than most people can ever imagine. Indeed, these are truly amazing people!

Those who have known great suffering often experience a paradox in relation to others. On the one hand, personal relationships frequently fall apart. On the other hand, the same intensity that seems to destroy the love of those closest to them is the same intensity that enables the survivor to demonstrate great compassion toward others. In a crisis, when things look the worst, these people seem to come alive with a calm and assurance that appears almost palpable. These are the caretakers, the loyalists, the in-charge folks. If I was on my deathbed, I would want one of these people by my side—he or she would know what to do.

Cultivating Compassion

One of my favorite and often overlooked stories in the life of Jesus is the account of his response to the death of John the Baptist. The disciples came to tell Jesus that his friend had been beheaded. Naturally, Jesus wanted some time alone so he got into a boat and set off for a quiet place. However, he wasn't the only one who was suffering. Those with loved ones who were ill followed after Jesus. And what was his response to them, out of the depths of his own anguish? "When Jesus landed and saw a large crowd, he had compassion on them and healed their sick" (Matthew 14:14). Mark adds that Jesus looked upon the people as being "like sheep without a shepherd" (Mark 6:34). In many ways this describes exactly what I see in those who have been so terribly betrayed in their childhood. These are people who have lived in hell. They know their way around. They know it in others when they see it, when they feel it. And they are full of compassion, often desiring to communicate a tenderness, a healing touch.

Sarah was a person who could express great compassion in the midst of the most difficult circumstances. Her struggle, however, to keep from categorizing every man as a sex monster was sometimes debilitating. She could make others pretty uneasy with some of her interpretations of the world. However, she could also become immediately focused on the care of another when everyone else seemed to be losing their heads and falling apart. She was a survivor. She had traveled the depths of hell. She knew her way around. She was cultivating compassion.

Breaking the Pattern of Dissociation

The best way that I know to break the pattern of dissociation is with a three-pronged approach that gives attention to physical, social, and cognitive elements in the process of integration.

I can't say enough about the importance of physical exercise in the process of healing dissociative disorders related to sexual abuse. Whether a person engages in the martial arts, yoga, weight training, or swimming, the effect of muscular contraction, increased heart rate and breathing, along with the mental discipline of routine will enhance a person's ability to gauge and control her body response systems. In addition, regular physical exercise reprograms the body's somatic memory and allows one to become more confident in following the body's normal (and positive) system changes to a variety of stimuli.

The best social environment for healing dissociation can be found in group therapy made up of participants with similar abuse experiences. There is nothing like someone who has been there to help keep a person honest. Reality testing is the key, as group members both challenge and support one another's consistency (or lack thereof) in their integration of thoughts, emotions, and corresponding behaviors. The basic idea here is that group members mirror back what they see, hear, and feel from the others as a way to check whether or not situations and responses are a good fit.

Finally, cognitive restructuring will be an invaluable part of the integrative process in healing dissociation. In other words, some of the person's core beliefs will need to be challenged and restructured to reflect a more accurate picture of reality that includes a strong concept of the person as a child of God with purpose and hope for the future. Often this cognitive work is best facilitated by individual therapy. Breaking the patterns of dissociation allows spiritual restoration to begin.

Prayer

Dearest Jesus,
I want to be "normal."
I want to be able to feel again.
I want to feel real joy . . . and so I know I must feel
*   the real pain.*
I am afraid.
Send your holy, helping, healing spirit.
I will open my heart, slowly. Slowly.
Amen.

"This cup that we drink, is it not a participation in the blood of Christ?" So goes Paul's explanation of the holy meal that we call Communion. This is no ordinary meal. This is a place where Jesus shows up to offer himself for the forgiveness of sins.

Kathryn approached the Table of the Lord with both respect and heightened anticipation. This was a place where she came to meet God. This was a place where the cup of blessing poured out immeasurable mercy toward her and her loved ones. This was a sacred place where renewal and restoration could begin to take hold.

CHAPTER FIVE

THE HEALING
POWER
OF CONFESSION
AND ABSOLUTION

Kathryn, age 34

Kathryn, a married mother of two, was one of the most religious people I have ever met. She was faithful at worship, sang in the choir, and volunteered as often as possible. In fact, she seemed so consumed with the idea of serving God that I began to wonder whether or not her activity level was healthy for her and her family.

As her pastor, I discussed my observations and concerns with Kathryn about her overcommitment. It certainly wasn't the case that Kathryn's efforts were becoming a problem to me. She was one of the most creative and dedicated people I knew. I could count on her for anything . . . perhaps too easily. One day Kathryn shared her story with me about how she had been sexually abused as a child and how God was doing a healing work in her life through a twelve-step support group. "God has been so good to me," she said, "that I just want to serve him with my whole life." And then Kathryn turned to me and said, "Maybe you need to have a greater heart for God yourself so that you would understand me better."

For several weeks, Kathryn appeared distant toward me. Normally she was readily at hand whenever I turned around. There had never been a shortage of opportunities to interact with Kathryn. But now, even though she was still active, Kathryn didn't get very close to me. I understood that my conversation with her may have caused her some discomfort, and that she probably needed time to process what was said. I decided not to push our relationship. Rather, I would wait for a while before approaching her again.

Finally, I decided to check in with Kathryn about our difficult conversation. "What did you think about what was said between us?" I asked. Kathryn responded, "I was hurt and embarrassed. I didn't want to hear what you were saying about my over-commitment. I never thought about my activities at church as being like an addiction or obsession." She continued, "But I talked about it at my support group and the feedback suggested that you were right. I don't know how to say no to people, especially if I think they might be disappointed in me." I told Kathryn that I was proud of the work she was doing in her support group, and I offered to help her learn how to say no to some of the activities at church. In many ways, just my permission seemed to provide relief.

Listening to Your Whole Body

As Kathryn and I talked together, I experienced the same strange feeling that I have had before in the presence of someone who has suffered sexual abuse. I felt as though Kathryn's body was separate from her head. Oh, I could see that they were physically connected, but it was as though each was a separate entity unto itself. It felt like there was a talking head on top of this prop called a body. I decided to follow my visceral lead and ask Kathryn about it. "That's amazing," she said. "I sometimes have a difficult time reading my own emotions. It's as though my head tells people yes, then later my body says no. I can feel very resentful and think that others are trying to take advantage of me, when actually it's just that I can't seem to say no.

This difficulty with saying no is certainly not unique to those who have been sexually abused (though the motivation to alleviate the feeling of shame can intensify the experience). However, the part that is unique is the detachment of the head from the body. And this is where the challenge of integrating the two is necessary for the sexually abused person to feel whole. For Kathryn this meant that she needed to check in with her accountability group, the twelve-step support group, and do some reality testing. Kathryn needed to begin to listen to her whole body.

Twelve-Step Programs and Confession and Absolution

It has been interesting to follow the growth in popularity of the various twelve-step programs. There is a program for almost every type of ailment, from the more familiar Alcoholics Anonymous to the rather obscure Disorganized Anonymous. For many, many people these programs work. What these programs have in common are the basic twelve steps, which originated with Alcoholics Anonymous.

The **first step** is crucial as it states, *I am powerless over* _____ (alcohol, sex, shopping, gambling, eating, disorganization, holding grudges, etc.). You fill in the blank. The **second step** states, *I believe that only a higher power can help me.* Depending on a person's faith perspective, this "higher power" takes on the image of what has traditionally been called "God." For the Christian, this would be clarified even further by referencing Jesus. But usually the twelve-step programs leave this definition up to the individual participants.

As a pastor, I'm struck by how similar the first two steps are to what we traditionally call Confession & Absolution. In the liturgy of many Protestant and Catholic churches the congregation often begins the service by saying:

(Confession = Step One)

Most merciful God, **we confess that we are in bondage to sin and cannot free ourselves**. We have sinned against you in thought, word, and deed, by what we have done and by what we have left undone. We have not loved you with our whole heart; we have not loved our neighbors as ourselves. For the sake of your Son, Jesus Christ, have mercy on us. Forgive us, renew us, and lead us, so that we may delight in your will and walk in your ways, to the glory of your holy name. Amen (*Lutheran Book of Worship*, p. 56, emphasis added).

Then the pastor follows with the words of absolution:

(Absolution = Step Two)

In the mercy of almighty God, **Jesus Christ was given to die for us**, and for his sake God forgives us all our sins. To those who believe in Jesus Christ **he gives the power to become the children of God and bestows on them the Holy Spirit** (*Lutheran Book of Worship*, p. 56, emphasis added).

Steps one and two are not exactly the same as confession and absolution, but they certainly are similar enough to draw some comparisons. Powerlessness over sin and the need for God's restorative power in our lives are classic Christian beliefs. The powerlessness can be equated with Original Sin (our fallen, broken nature, as in Psalm 51:5), while the need for restoration can be found in our Lord's Word of forgiveness and Holy Sacraments of Baptism and Communion. In fact, I would suggest that gathering for Christian worship is in many ways like one holy twelve-step meeting! The difference is that we more clearly identify who the "Higher Power" is, namely, God the Father, Son, and Holy Spirit.

The Power of Personal Confession and Absolution

In my experience it is very beneficial for each person to become more specific in his or her prayers of confession. My parishioners and counseling clients have taught me that it is important that they name their own deep sense of brokenness and that they confess their own personal emotions and actions. Unfortunately, we don't tend to model this specificity in our Sunday worship. The statement of confession is general, often corporate ("forgive us" instead of "forgive me"). And while there is benefit in such general and corporate prayers ("we're all in this together"), I wonder how deeply our brokenness and desperate need for God is felt and understood at a personal level.

Someone might suggest that leading a person who has been sexually abused toward confession and absolution is at best insensitive and at worst destructive. In other words, how could I encourage a person to feel bad about herself when she already feels so bad? My response is that the experience of confession normalizes life for the abused. She knows that she is in need of God's intervention just like everyone else. She is keenly aware of the fact that she blows it on a regular basis. Her love toward God and others is not what it should be. Therefore, standing alongside everyone else, she acknowledges her need and receives the comforting word of mercy and forgiveness.

In my experience, one of the great misconceptions among those who work with the sexually abused is the idea that confession will only compound the victim's misery. Paradoxically, I find just the opposite, namely, that the abused appreciates the opportunity to express doubt, fear, anger, disappointment, even contempt toward God and her neighbor. She is then prepared to receive the soothing balm of the Gospel message, which assures her of God's love because of the suffering, death, and resurrection of his son, Jesus. It is only in feeling the strength of this forgiveness that the abused is then able to "Go in peace and serve the Lord."

Martin Luther, in *The Bondage of the Will,* provides an illustration of how God works mercy in our lives to restore and heal. Luther says that God demands perfection from everyone. God also knows that such perfection is impossible because of our sinfulness. For God to demand such perfection, Luther says, is analogous to a man without any legs sitting in a chair and someone saying to him, "Get up and walk!"

This command to get up and walk would be cruel and insensitive given the man's obvious limitations. God, however, does this very thing when he demands perfection. The result is that we are forced to look more clearly at ourselves and our inability. We are then prepared to cry out for God's mercy at which point our hearts have been prepared to receive what we need. God comes to us, then, with mercy and grace in Word and Sacrament, picks us up and carries us into faith and forgiveness. God sets us down and calls us dear sons and daughters. Now the healing can begin.

There is something powerful and healing about the physicality of the Sacraments. Baptism has water that you can see and hear and feel. The Lord's Supper has a cup with wine or grape juice that you can see and feel, smell and taste. As part of the spiritual restoration process it is important for the one who has been abused to experience a positive physical presence associated with God. Like the disciple Thomas, it helps reinforce the reality of God's presence when we can see and touch and hold life in our hands.

The Lord's Supper and Sacred Ritual

Kathryn was especially sensitive to her participation at the Lord's Supper. The body broken and the blood shed was a constant reminder of her Lord's love for her. "Every time I receive this bread and wine, I think of Jesus suffering on the cross. I can see him there hanging, bleeding, gasping, dying. I feel great sorrow for him since he didn't deserve such a death. He was innocent, perfect, and spotless. Someone once said that if I was the only person on earth, Jesus would have died for me. He must love me very much."

We discussed how Jesus, the Son of God, could have called upon thousands of angels to rescue him from the cross, but that he chose death instead. In the New Testament letter to the Hebrews, the author describes what Jesus was thinking as he suffered on the cross. "For the joy set before [Jesus] endured the cross, scorning its shame" (Hebrews 12:2). In other words, Jesus was able to look beyond his present suffering and imagine the possibility of something better, a healing and wholeness and return to his Father that would fill him with joy unspeakable. It was this kind of hope that I wished for Kathryn. And somehow during her participation at the Lord's Supper, she received a foretaste of the things to come, the joy that is unspeakable.

I really can't overstate the importance of sacred ritual in our lives. By ritual, I don't mean something dead and lifeless. Rather, I'm talking about those times when we mark our lives with the sacred, the Holy. A regular time of prayer and reading Scripture is a great example of how we mark our lives with God's presence. Baptism and the Lord's Supper are further examples of how we recognize our need for God-at-work in our lives. Somehow the ordinary rituals of brushing teeth, checking e-mail, and driving to work need to be offset by seeing God come to us from outside of ourselves. And whether our struggle is with alcohol, sex, disorganization, or sabotaging relationships, we all need to be reminded of God's presence to heal and restore our relationship with him.

Prayer

Dearest Jesus,
I confess _____.
I confess _____.
I confess_____.
I ask your forgiveness.
I am so grateful for your compassion and love
*   toward me.*
I am so grateful for the Holy Spirit, the breath of God
*   moving in me.*
Thank you for your real, abiding, and healing presence
*   in my life.*
Amen.

There is no greater picture of intimacy than of two people holding hands. But which hand is doing the holding and which hand is being held? Exactly! Both are holding and being held at the same time. There can be no divisiveness here. It's hard to fight while holding hands.

This picture, "Friends," is the foundation of marriage, and David understood this as well as anyone I have ever met. Marriage is an expression of mutual consent, of risk-taking and refuge. And the message is clear . . . we are together, side-by-side. Not one in front and the other behind . . . but side-by-side.

CHAPTER SIX

FRIENDSHIP

David, age 55

David was an Accounts Executive for a large, multibillion-dollar company. He called me for counseling because he was concerned that his marriage was having trouble. I requested that both he and his wife attend counseling together for several weekly sessions, which they agreed to do.

David and his wife, Carol, were both previously married and each had children from those marriages. They also shared two children together, and they had managed to stay in touch with their large family pretty well. All of their children were adults; a couple of them were married and starting families of their own. As complicated as these family dynamics were, David and Carol enjoyed a fairly settled life. Over the past two years, however, this couple had begun to experience an increasing emotional distance between them. David was spending more time at work and the couple rarely had sexual relations.

Was David going through a mid-life crisis? Had Carol begun menopause? Maybe David was depressed and feeling a lack of job security. With the children grown and gone, maybe Carol was reevaluating her place in the world. Maybe David was experiencing impotence and therefore withdrawing from Carol. Possibly all of these issues could be factored into our discussion and, as usual, I explored each one. It wasn't until we had been in counseling for a couple of months, however, that Carol said, "I think David's past sexual abuse may have something to do with our problems." I glanced back quickly at the intake form and the life history questionnaire. Nothing had been reported about childhood sexual abuse. There was a place on the original intake form for this information, but David did not supply it. Where did this come from? And why hadn't

I asked the question already? Would I have caught this earlier if David had been a woman?

Up to this point in this book I have focused only on women who have suffered childhood sexual abuse. The five examples leading up to the story of David reflect my personal counseling experience. That is, I hear of sexual abuse from women about five times more than I hear from men. I really don't know how accurate that ratio is in relation to actual numbers. Certainly women still seek therapy in general more readily than men, which could account for the skewing of numbers. It may be that men are more reluctant to talk about sexual abuse. As I discuss in my book, *I Love You, Son: What Every Boy (and Man) Needs to Hear,* many men simply haven't learned a language for a wide range of emotional expression and may not know how to talk about what they are feeling. But the truth is, many men have been victims of childhood sexual abuse, and the long-term, destructive ramifications have been great whether conscious or not.

David had been sexually abused as a child, and it was just within the past couple of years that he had begun to remember this more fully. I asked him to recount what he could remember and he told me about being at a community swimming pool at the age of ten. An older man followed him into the bathhouse where he performed oral sex on David. David said, "I just froze up. My body went numb. I didn't know what to do or to say. I really didn't understand what had just happened. All I knew was that the man told me that if I said anything he would kill my family. I never spoke a word of it to anyone until just recently to Carol and now to you."

But how was Carol able to make the connection between David's abuse and their problems as a couple? Turns out,

Carol had also been sexually abused as a child and David's recent revelation had begun to stir up old emotions within her about her own experiences. Now we had two deeply wounded individuals, both of whom had managed to be very successful in many areas of their lives. But the bubble was beginning to burst. The protective shields were starting to crumble and they seriously questioned whether or not either one could withstand the pain of addressing their past hurts and remaining together at the same time. As Carol said, "I just don't know if I can allow David to get close to me again. His recent withdrawal from me has brought back terrible feelings of shame and rejection. I'm overwhelmed most of the time now." We were obviously embarking on a long and difficult journey.

David suffered from dysthymia, a pervasive, low-grade depression. He needed an antidepressant, preferably Wellbutrin as this often has the added benefit of an increased libido for many people. Paradoxically, though, we would need to introduce desensitization techniques since his sexual reaction was to freeze his body (a reenactment of his childhood sexual abuse experience). With drug therapy, David would have the strength needed to begin addressing his past abuse and its affects on his current marriage.

You Are God's Beloved

David enjoyed reading and expressed a desire for a closer relationship with God. I recommended Henri Nouwen's book *Life of the Beloved,* based upon four marks or characteristics that describe the life of the Beloved (one who is loved by God). Nouwen's four-fold schema of "Taken (or Chosen), Blessed, Broken, and Given" follows the language of the Lord's Supper. These four themes are each applied to the individual in this sequence starting with "Taken (or Chosen)." After reading the book, David exclaimed, "I can't seem to get past the Taken (or Chosen) part. I have a very difficult time with the idea that I am chosen by God unconditionally as my whole life is based upon competition." He then read the following from Nouwen:

> Self-rejection is the greatest enemy of the spiritual life because it contradicts the sacred voice that calls us the Beloved. . . . I am putting this so directly and so simply because, though the experience of being the Beloved has never been completely absent from my life, I never claimed it as my core truth. I kept running around it in large or small circles, always looking for someone or something able to convince me of my Belovedness. It was as if I kept refusing to hear the voice that speaks from the very depth of my being and says: "You are my Beloved, on you my favor rests." That voice has always been there, but it seems that I was much more eager to listen to other, louder voices saying: "Prove that you are worth something; do something relevant, spectacular, or powerful, and then you will earn the love you so desire." Meanwhile, the soft, gentle voice that speaks in the silence and solitude of my heart remained unheard or, at least, unconvincing (pp. 28-29).

As with most of the people that I see in counseling, it is often important and helpful for us to spend some time talking about God's original will for the creation. We have to go back before the fall, before the rebellion of human beings got set in motion. Back there we find a perfect world of God's design, a world without destruction, chaos, heartache, and death. No abuse, no such thing as victims and perpetrators. Only a God whose character of love could be seen imprinted in all of the creation. And God looked upon all that was made and said, "It is very good." Every human being, every creature, and every product of nature had intrinsic value and worth coming from the hand of its creator. For David, this meant that he needed to see himself with God's eyes, without rejection, as "very good."

Certainly we all bear the marks of our brokenness and fallenness. Truly much has gone wrong with God's original creation. And thankfully God so loved the creation that God sent Jesus to begin the restoration process that will culminate with the return of our Lord at the end of time. However, even now we need to gain a glimpse of the "very-goodness" inherent in God's creation. And with God's help, we can (David could) begin to see the marks of reversal that signal the powerful presence of God recreating our spirits, our hearts, our minds, our whole lives.

Friendship

When David and Carol began to see themselves more as God's Beloved, they began to cultivate a true friendship. David and Carol began to hold hands and walk together again. They began to see their need, especially in this latter half of life, for both dependency and support. Like the picture at the beginning of this chapter, "Friendship" was the key to their healing process. And in their friendship they rediscovered some of the "very-goodness" of God's creation.

Zig Zigler, the famous motivational speaker, is probably best known for his book, *How To Win Friends and*

Influence People. While this book has much that I would commend, the very title has the ring of corporate manipulation that makes me feel uncomfortable when it comes to discussing the basis for true friendship.

One of the best images of true friendship is the image of Jesus kneeling down to wash his disciples' feet. This action was one of great humility on the part of Jesus. Surely he had every right to expect that others would wash his feet. But instead, he took on the humble role of a servant, bowed down, and lovingly cared for the needs of others. No pride. No shame. No explanation. Just a humble act.

The power of friendship can be seen and felt most powerfully in acts of humility. I am more willing to be vulnerable in the presence of another when he or she has demonstrated vulnerability with me. I can readily share my weaknesses when I see that those around me understand their own weaknesses and are quick to acknowledge them. Like stepping down to wash another person's feet, the movement down is so much easier than the movement up.

I don't want to go through life always feeling that I have to live-up, measure-up, one-up. My breathing becomes constricted at high altitudes. Rather, I want to move and breathe in a comfortable place. I need to feel refreshed by my relationships, not torn in two. Again the image of walking hand-in-hand is a good one in that it reinforces our togetherness. Not one in front and the other behind, but both side-by-side.

I don't think true healing and spiritual restoration are possible without vulnerability. We have to allow another to get close enough to see us for who we really are with the hope that he or she will want to stick around after they see us more fully. This tenderness, this acceptance conveys the message that we are worth the trouble. And we open our wounds in this environment of acceptance and begin to feel restored.

Prayer

Dearest Jesus,
I need a friend.
I need to be a friend.
I need someone who will walk hand-in-hand with me.
I need someone who knows what it is like to be abused.
Take my hand, Jesus.
I will take yours.
Amen.

PART TWO

STORIES

OF NEW LIFE

CHAPTER SEVEN

LAZARUS AND THE RICH MAN: A STORY OF RESTORATION

What, if anything, does the parable of Lazarus and the Rich Man have to do with child sexual abuse? On the surface this parable doesn't appear to have any immediate application to our subject. However, in this story Jesus demonstrates a profound understanding and compassion for those who suffer unjustly. Through this parallel we are able to draw our applications.

The Story

There was a rich man who was dressed in purple and fine linen and lived in luxury every day. At his gate was laid a beggar named Lazarus, covered with sores and longing to eat what fell from the rich man's table. Even the dogs came and licked his sores.

The time came when the beggar died and the angels carried him to Abraham's side. The rich man also died and was buried. In hell, where he was in torment, he looked up and saw Abraham far away, with Lazarus by his side. So he called to him, "Father Abraham, have pity on me and send Lazarus to dip the tip of his finger in water and cool my tongue, because I am in agony in this fire."

But Abraham replied, "Son, remember that in your lifetime you received your good things, while Lazarus received bad things, but now he is comforted here and you are in agony. And besides all this, between us and you a great chasm has been fixed, so that those who want to go from here to you cannot, nor can anyone cross over from there to us."

He answered, "Then I beg you, father, send Lazarus to my father's house, for I have five brothers. Let him warn them, so that they will not also come to this place of torment."

Abraham replied, "They have Moses and the Prophets; let them listen to them."

"No, father Abraham," he said, "but if someone from the dead goes to them, they will repent."

He said to him, "If they do not listen to Moses and the Prophets, they will not be convinced even if someone rises from the dead" (Luke 16:19-31).

In this parable, I see three distinct stages of movement, namely Pre-Death, Death, and New Life. These three stages form the basis of my thought as I attempt to draw some parallels between the experience of one who has been victimized through child sexual abuse and the suffering of Lazarus.

Pre-Death

There was a rich man who was dressed in purple and fine linen and lived in luxury every day. At his gate was laid a beggar named Lazarus, covered with sores and longing to eat what fell from the rich man's table. Even the dogs came and licked his sores.

The backdrop of this story presents a stark contrast between a rich man and a poor man. One is covered in purple (the color of royalty), while the other is covered with sores (not only a beggar, but a very sick one at that). What could be more repulsive than to have the rich man's gate littered with the stench of this man who could do nothing but lie in the way? Did people have to walk past him to enter the gate? Why didn't the rich man at least have the man removed from the premises? Wouldn't that have been preferred for everyone, including the beggar?

"At his gate was laid." This is the passive voice. The man can't walk. Who puts him in his place each day? Other beggars? Or people with means? Why don't they give him something to eat instead of leaving him at the gate? Perhaps they feel that someone else, someone with greater financial ability should care for this down-and-outer (literally down and, now, out of the way).

Lazarus . . . oh, this beggar has a name. But in his condition, who cares about a name? Let's stick with "poor beggar." It's easier to digest, less personal that way. And he waits for crumbs to fall from the rich man's table. Patience? No. What else can he do but wait? And he wouldn't think of moving much even if he could because he is covered with sores (unclean by anyone's standards). And what of the dogs? Has this man who waits for crumbs become a meal for the dogs himself? His entire body weeps.

Not many of us, especially in North America, can relate to the picture presented here. Most of us have a hard time relating to the helplessness, the immobility, and the physical pain both internal and external. And what of the mental anguish—no better than food for a dog. Certainly the stench must have been unbearable, with people shuffling past and through the gate, careful not to touch him.

When I share this story with one who has been sexually abused, however, there is an immediate connection, a recognizable helplessness and pain. And often one of the first responses by the abused is, "Where was God for this man? For me?" Next comes the weeping and a deep, thick, tremor-like shaking. The sores have broken open once again.

As I sit with this one who is in so much pain, I want
to reach out and hold her. I want her to know that she's
not alone. But then, I could never fully understand. I've
never been sexually abused. And would she experience
my touch—that of a man—as comforting or threaten-
ing? Now I am afraid. I want to move quickly past the
pain, through the gate, and into the palace of luxury.
Going home today will carry new meaning for me.

Everyone who was supposed to help, protect, and
nurture this one so abused has let her down. She was just
left "at the gate," passive, afraid, without resources to care
for herself. And she became both food and stench for the
dogs. Life, mere existence, had no good purpose. How
does a child survive, let alone thrive, in such an environment? "I wonder where the poor beggar escaped to in
his mind to relieve the suffering," the woman says as she
sits in front of me, her body turned slightly to my right
and eyes looking into the distance. This is not a time for
direct communication.

Death

*The time came when the beggar died and the angels carried
him to Abraham's side. The rich man also died and was buried. In hell, where he was in torment, he looked up and saw
Abraham far away, with Lazarus by his side. So he called to
him, "Father Abraham, have pity on me and send Lazarus to
dip the tip of his finger in water and cool my tongue, because
I am in agony in this fire."*

"The time came when the beggar died." Finally, death
comes to us all—true relief from all of the sorrow. And

Lazarus certainly was familiar with sorrow. Perhaps this is how he will be remembered by those who buried him—a man of sorrows. Can't you just see the people walking past the burial site and telling their friends about the man who used to lie at the rich man's gate and beg for food? He was kind of a novelty, a strange attraction of sorts. Poor fool.

What of this poor beggar's death? As the rich man's servants carried the lifeless body of Lazarus outside the city gates (only the privileged of society were buried inside the city), they had no idea that his soul was being carried by angels to Abraham's side. Indeed, this poor beggar had experienced the great reversal at the end. This is a true rags-to-riches story if ever there was one—and this one ends with eternity.

As I sit with one who has experienced childhood sexual abuse, I hear a connection being made with the question of how he or she will be remembered after death. Will people only remember the sorrow or will they see triumph and victory over the afflictions of the abuse? So many people only see a troubled soul. They don't understand why the soul is troubled, secretly suffering, hidden in terror, full of a demoralizing shame.

The image of Lazarus being carried by the angels to Abraham's side (literally "bosom") is one of safety and nurture. Oh, how the abused longs to feel this kind of human/divine touch. Even the disciple, John, rested on the bosom of Jesus. Why must this be sexualized? Why can't we in the West accept this tenderness with a sacred trust? How tragic it is when those who abuse their powers destroy not only the soul of an individual but also the gift of touch for a whole society.

Abraham himself knew what it meant to trust God. He had set out on a journey by faith to a new home where

God would lead him. He understood what it felt like to leave the security of the familiar and wander aimlessly with only the inner assurance that God was already out ahead of him preparing a place for him to abide. I think of the abused with whom I sit in this room. I pray, "God, grant the strength of your presence to this one before me, alongside of me, who needs to feel at home in his or her own body and mind."

"The rich man also died and was buried." Surely this was a spectacular event. Imagine the mourners who gathered around to pay their last respects. This was a man of power, wealth, and great position. Any wrong-doing in his life must be overshadowed by his achievements. Only a proper burial for this man . . . what was his name? The text does not give him a name. He would be buried within the city gates with a monument for a tombstone. And the epitaph would read, "He lived a full life." But now he is "in hell" . . . "in torment." Eternal life has already begun. Is it a resting place? Not for this man. God has avenged poor Lazarus at last.

Frequently I hear from the abused a common fantasy that the perpetrator has died and can no longer threaten anyone else. I hear of deep hatred and seething revenge. "Damn them," they cry. And it all makes perfect sense. Even better is what comes next in our story as the rich man (now no longer rich) "looked up and saw Abraham far away, with Lazarus by his side." For the first time in his life the man looked up to seek help. And who does he see but Lazarus beside Abraham "far away." This is the kind of distance that the abused desires. Even in death, perhaps especially in death, there needs to be a place of safety. How unnerving it is when the perpetrator can be heard to speak even from the grave. The child (now adult) carries the image, the voice, the smell of the perpetrator. No distance, not even death, seems far enough.

The man called out, "Father Abraham, have pity on me and send Lazarus to dip the tip of his finger in water and cool my tongue, because I am in agony in this fire." Lazarus can see the tables have been turned. He is in the palace and the other man is at the gate begging. For the one who has been abused, this is a critical point in the journey toward health. When the perpetrator is seen as one who is impoverished, destitute, and pathetic, the abused can begin to feel the distance between them. The name *Lazarus* means, "God has helped," signifying that God has intervened. Alongside of Abraham (a counselor, a friend) there is safety, peace, and rest.

New Life

Let's look at the story closely to see the New Life that emerges.

But Abraham replied, "Son, remember that in your life-time you received your good things, while Lazarus received bad things, but now he is comforted here and you are in agony. And besides all this, between us and you a great chasm has been fixed, so that those who want to go from here to you cannot, nor can anyone cross over from there to us."

He answered, "Then I beg you, father, send Lazarus to my father's house, for I have five brothers. Let him warn them, so that they will not also come to this place of torment."

Good and evil are realigned

"You received your good things, while Lazarus received bad things." Good and evil have now been reversed . . . corrected. For the longest time the abused has felt out of sync with his or her emotions. The perpetrator, the trusted one, taught that evil is good, and good is evil. This confusion between what is good and what is evil is an ongoing struggle. But for the abused, recognizing the perpetrator's insidious reversal is a healthy rebellion. Reality testing ("Am I really feeling what I think I'm feeling?"), and integration of head, heart, and hands all move the abused toward wholeness.

Genuine comfort prevails

"But now he is comforted." Suddenly in the story we see a new feeling, a new life in the present. The abused is no longer the victim. She has moved from surviving to thriving. A feeling of genuine comfort prevails. God has moved this person to a new place that is in relationship with God and with others. Feelings of community and connection have taken over where loneliness once prevailed.

The perpetrator is no longer a threat

"A great chasm has been fixed." The perpetrator is still alive—at a distance—but no real threat. With this realization I often hear the abused say, "I'm moving on with my life. I'm learning to love myself and another." Finally the struggle has resulted in a newfound dignity. Love, God's love, really does cast out fear.

There is no going back

"Send Lazarus." Lazarus himself cannot go back, and the abused doesn't want to be exposed to the power of the perpetrator. But their story needs to be told so that others may be spared. Compassion for the most vulnerable is a mark of genuine health. Those who have been abused will often say, "I don't know if I can ever forgive the perpetrator. Only God can do that. But I can tell my story."

The Marks of Spiritual Restoration

These four marks of the New Life are consistent with spiritual restoration for the sexually abused.

1) Good and evil have been realigned. The individual has gained confidence in her ability to distinguish between good and evil, even within herself.

2) A new and dominant feeling of genuine comfort prevails. How the present is now experienced provides hope for the future.

3) The perpetrator is no longer perceived as a threat. Love for self (based upon God's love for his creation) has replaced the shame.

4) There is no going back. The road of spiritual restoration has been traveled far enough to trust that God is guiding the way. Forgiveness for the perpetrator is placed in God's hands.

In the remaining chapters I'd like to shift our attention to some people who have traveled the road of spiritual restoration from Pre-Death to Death and onto New Life. In varying degrees, the following people demonstrate the emergence of the four marks of the New Life as described above. Their stories give hope to those who are still in the first two stages of Pre-Death and Death. And while the experience of abuse is and always will be a part of their lives, for those who have moved toward spiritual restoration the abuse is only a part instead of the whole definition of who they are. They are renewed children of God. They are beloved by God and feel the assurance of God's presence in their lives. They feel safe in God's embrace and confident of the Holy Spirit's indwelling.

A kiss given in tenderness and love is a child's assurance that she is valued and needed in this world. With a hand on her mother's mouth the child signals an innate knowledge that nourishment is intended to come from these lips.

Amber made an important discovery about her relationship with God that found its greatest expression during Holy Communion. As God nourished her through eating and drinking, by giving the assurance of his presence in the touch of her mouth, so Amber began to extend this blessing of God's presence to her own child in the form of a kiss.

CHAPTER EIGHT

THE LOOP
OF INTIMACY

Amber, age 35

Amber was a delight to be around. Everyone who met her loved her. She had a gift for affirming people and making them feel special in the eyes of God. And she had been sexually abused as a child.

I was impressed by Amber the first time I met her. She spoke with a grace that betrayed the kind of spiritual depth that comes from gratitude toward God for providing the most basic things of life. She didn't take anything for granted. Her life, marriage, and family were precious to her. And she loved her quiet time with God during which she would be reminded of God's love for her. Her greatest concern, and the reason she came to see me, was that lately Amber was having a difficult time allowing her husband to get close to her sexually. They had three children and had enjoyed an active sex life in the past, but recently she was shutting down in response to her husband's advances.

I asked Amber if there had been any significant changes in her life recently. She responded that the family had just moved here from out of state about six months ago. Everyone was ready to move and felt good about the change and so it didn't seem relevant to her difficulty with sharing intimacy. Amber was concerned that issues from past abuse might be showing up creating a barrier between her and her husband. So we explored the concept of intimacy together.

The Loop of Intimacy is a tool that I use with individuals and couples to help them diagnose their level of difficulty with the movement between emotional closeness and emotional distance. Usually after introducing and explaining the Loop, those who are motivated to be self-reflective will readily identify where they are on the Loop and how they move from one emotional stage to the other. Let's take a closer look at the Loop of Intimacy.

The Loop of Intimacy

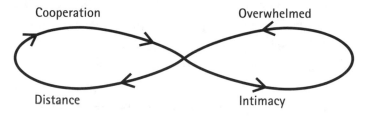

Cooperation | Overwhelmed

Distance | Intimacy

A couple begins at the first emotional stage, Cooperation, before moving on to Intimacy. Cooperation could be any activity that is done together, like planning a trip or planting a garden. It doesn't really matter what the activity is as long as it includes mutually supportive, give-and-take time together. In other words, the couple isn't watching a video together nor is the couple spending "parallel" time together (parallel time is when a couple may be in the same house, even the same room, but each one is devoted to separate interests). There must be sustained, ongoing interaction in order for the stage to be considered Cooperation.

Once a couple has experienced the stage of Cooperation in a mutually supportive way, they eventually begin to move toward the stage of Intimacy. Intimacy, as used here, is not to be equated with sex. Sex can certainly be a part of intimacy, but intimacy is a much larger, foundational part of the relationship. In other words, true intimacy occurs first and foremost outside of the bedroom.

"The ability to share pain" is the best way that I have found to define intimacy. Pain in this sense refers to vulnerabilities, fears, dashed hopes, faded dreams, and disappointments in self and others. The freedom to share this pain is the glue that holds a marriage together. The skill of listening to understand, rather than to fix or criticize, is key in establishing an environment of trust. The level of trust and security that a couple feels together is directly related to their level of disclosure.

Intimacy as defined here is a very intense experience. At this stage there is a connectedness that begins to define the scriptural image of a husband and wife becoming "one flesh" (Genesis 2:24). Like peeling off layers of clothing, each time a couple moves around the Loop they expose a little more. Again, sex may occur at this stage, but not necessarily. (However, men, when your wife says she doesn't feel ready for sex, it's probably because you haven't spent enough time at the stage of Cooperation. This may be especially true for one who has experienced childhood sexual abuse.)

No one can stand to remain at any one emotional stage on the Loop indefinitely. There has to be movement (note the directional arrows on the Loop). This means that Intimacy eventually gives way to the feeling that I call Overwhelmed. This stage represents the intensity of closeness that becomes smothering, even oppressive. At this time there needs to be some movement toward the emotional stage called Distance to allow each person the opportunity to take a deep breath and experience the feeling of being a separate individual.

This stage of Distance is not a "stepping away from" the relationship. No one steps out of the Loop. There simply seems to be a need for some self-reflective time (reading a book, riding a bike, taking a walk) before re-engaging more fully at the stage of Cooperation and thus beginning the Loop all over again.

Distance will be achieved consciously or unconsciously. If unconsciously, distance will likely occur with a flare up between a couple at a time when everything seemed to be going well. However, a couple can learn to make this movement more conscious by recognizing that the subtle irritations that eventually accompany intense closeness are a signal that the couple is beginning to feel overwhelmed and needs some distance or time alone.

Some people (most often women) will feel threatened by the experience of this stage called Distance because they are afraid this means the end of closeness or Intimacy. Actually, it's helpful to see that the loop is continuous and that all four emotional stages are necessary.

Others (most often men) feel threatened by the experience of Intimacy. This is due in part because they haven't learned a language for emotions and also because they tend to operate with a narrow definition of the concept of Intimacy that restricts its use to the bedroom. For example, a number of women have told me that they never hear the words "I love you" except during lovemaking.

For the person who has been sexually abused, whether male or female, the otherwise natural movement from Cooperation to Intimacy can be easily circumvented so that a couple gets stuck in a cycle of Cooperation and Distance.

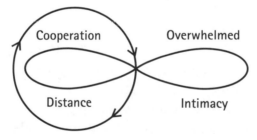

This was the case for Amber and her husband. What surprised Amber was that she had experienced so much healing around issues of intimacy that this Cooperation/ Distance cycle came as a big surprise. What she hadn't anticipated were the feelings that would flood back to her when her own daughter turned six.

Amber, herself, was six-years-old when she was first molested. Now, as her daughter turned six, Amber began to experience sleep problems, general fatigue, and an overall irritability. Increasingly she would lash out at her husband, whom she loved, without any apparent provocation. He was beside himself trying to understand her. And she was troubled since she seemed to make good starts at Cooperation only to pull back toward Distance when her husband began to show any interest in closeness. What Amber needed to see was that she had so closely identified with her daughter that she was getting emotionally stuck back at age six.

I asked Amber to write her daughter an age-appropriate letter telling her how she felt about her along with her expectations and dreams for her future. Then I asked her to read this letter aloud to her daughter and take her on a special outing, just the two of them. This exercise seemed to help Amber get unstuck as she realized that her daughter was safe and thriving in her (and her husband's) care. Shortly afterward, Amber reported feeling much closer to her husband and able to move toward intimacy for a sustained period of time.

The reason why this simple letter-writing exercise worked so profoundly was because Amber was relatively healthy in relation to her abuse issues. If it had been a couple of years earlier, the same approach probably wouldn't have been very helpful. But Amber had been enjoying a good level of intimacy with her husband and knew that he had her best interests at heart. It was for this very reason that Amber was so surprised by her feelings of withdrawal. This example shows that the abuse never really goes away, but it also shows that true healing can occur and so-called relapses can be dealt with and worked through much more quickly.

After the letter-writing experience, I noticed that Amber began giving her daughter a kiss at the altar whenever she came to communion. It became ceremonial, as though the pastor had said, "And now you may kiss your child." At one point I asked Amber about the kiss. She responded that the sacrament of Holy Communion was a time to reflect on God's love for her through the broken body of Christ. With this brokenness she felt that God poured out on her his undeserved and unconditional forgiveness and love. Amber simply wanted her daughter to make a healthy and positive connection between suffering and love. "My daughter needs to know that God understands her difficulties in this life and that he loves her. I guess the kiss is an opportunity for me to remind myself of the same thing, namely, that I am God's child whom he understands and loves."

I learned something from Amber about the power of the Sacrament of Holy Communion that I had never heard about during my seminary years. During seminary we spent most of our time parsing words and studying historical debates. I had no idea that such a seemingly simple, meditative gathering around an altar could provide the depth of healing that Amber taught me. Oh sure, I knew what the scriptures said about the power of the sacrament. But Amber helped me to see the Word made flesh. And the next time I went to communion, I kissed my daughter.

Prayer

Gracious God,
Thank you for your intimacy.
It sometimes scares me but I am grateful.
Thank you for staying with me.
Thank you for your mother's kiss.
Thank you for your unconditional love.
Amen.

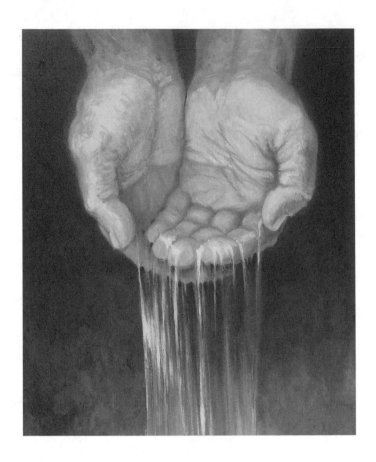

Water is a powerful substance. Too much or too little can kill. But in the right hands, water is a precious gift of life. It sustains and nourishes, soothes and delights. It quenches the strongest thirst.

In the picture above we find two cupped hands pouring water for all to drink. Thirst is the only requirement. This image also suggests the gift of Holy Baptism that brings new life and renewal. Jennifer desired such renewal and, through the death and resurrection of Jesus, she found it.

CHAPTER NINE

THE CYCLE

OF GRIEF

Jennifer, age 43

Jennifer was the wife of a career military man whom she met when he was stationed in Germany. They had two sons, ages sixteen and nineteen, and had been living back in the United States for about ten years. Jennifer came to me because of a profound, clinical depression following the discovery that her husband was having an affair.

The marriage had always been difficult due to the husband's sustained absences and emotional distance. In fact, there seemed to be an ironic correlation between Jennifer's increasing adaptability to living in the states and her husband's withdrawal. It was as if he could feel closer to his wife only when she relied upon him for everything. This, of course, was a pseudo-closeness that required more of a parent-child dependence. The affair gave Jennifer the motivation she needed to stand up to her husband, who had oppressed her personal opinions and preferences. Now he had committed the ultimate betrayal.

Certainly marital infidelity is troubling enough without throwing any other hardships into the mix. However, this betrayal by her husband opened up a deeper, older wound. At the age of fifteen, Jennifer had been raped by a "close friend of the family." Sadly Jennifer's husband added insult to injury by suggesting that his infidelity was a response to her distance. He claimed that he felt shut out by Jennifer due to the effects of the childhood rape. At this point it was important for the three of us to make a distinction between reasons and excuses, and to hold the husband responsible for his own actions. "You may feel that you have reasons for developing a relationship with another woman," I said, "but there is never an excuse for infidelity." This approach holds the man responsible for his actions while at the same time recognizes that there may be issues in the marriage that need to be addressed.

Jennifer's dual experience of betrayal made her counseling experience very complex. Both issues, the past rape and the current affair, needed attention. Fortunately, Jennifer had already done a great deal of work with a therapist in Germany on the issues related to the rape. But nothing had prepared her for how deeply she felt the connection between the past and present betrayals. Her grieving was at times unbearable. She was in torment and needed someone to accompany her on her journey through grief.

The Cycle of Grief

I often find it helpful to discuss the cycle of grief as a way to provide road-marks for the spiritual restoration process. It is important to remember that Jennifer had already done some significant healing work; otherwise she wouldn't have been able to move into an educational mode as quickly as she did. The following is the cycle of grief with explanation.

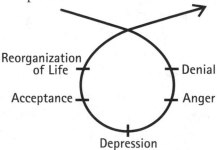

The above image is simple but not simplistic. It is also natural and normal, not unnatural or abnormal. Most often we think of the grieving process in relation to the death of a loved one and certainly that is a time for profound grieving. Over the years, however, we have discovered that the same type of grieving process has a much broader application to the experience of loss in general. Whether it be the loss of a job, a physical ability, or even the loss of a dream, hope, or expectation, the grieving process is the same and has a way of showing up in various degrees. Such was the case with Jennifer in relation to her past rape and current betrayal by her husband.

Jennifer had already struggled through much of the pain associated with the past rape. She recalled how she had deeply felt denial, anger, and depression, yet God had done an amazing healing work in her life around these intense emotions. Looking back, Jennifer could see that the stage called Denial was not a refusal to believe that she had been raped. She knew she had been raped. The denial was more of an inability or unwillingness to fully see the effects of the rape on her life, namely her view of herself and the world. Next in her journey of dealing with the rape, she began to take a closer look at the affects of the rape on her relationships with others. At that point Jennifer remembers experiencing an overwhelming anger. It was as though her eyes had been opened more fully to see the affects of the rape and she was outraged at what she saw. She admits that denial probably served an important function initially by allowing her to absorb what had happened to her in small, manageable increments. But by the time she started dealing with the rape issues, she had been stuck at the point of denial too long. As she was moving into the stages of Anger and Depression, flare-ups between her and her husband were what brought her into therapy while in Germany.

The Stair-Steps of Grief

It appears that we need to go through these stages of the cycle of grief as part of a natural, even restorative, process. Knowing this may not make the experience any easier. However, it helps to know that there is a normal progression and that eventually we will experience some forward movement. In fact, we usually go through a type of spiraling, stair-step motion in which we revisit our grief with an increasing ability to manage difficult emotions.

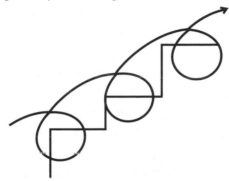

Once Jennifer moved emotionally from Denial to Anger, she was ready to go on to Depression. This depression does not need to be severe or clinical in nature, though it could be. And it may be helpful to find a different word to use such as sadness, loss of energy, lack of sustained focus, absence of delight, or even hopelessness and despair. The main point is that we often need to go through this stage as a hinge to move toward the other side of the cycle of grief (note the cycle of grief image, p. 103). In Jennifer's case, she began to accept that the rape was indeed a part of her life, but only one part of it. She also came to realize that the rape was also something that she could increasingly reference in the past. This emotional movement let her know that she was on her way toward the stage of Acceptance.

The Last Stage of the Cycle of Grief

You can see from the cycle of grief illustration (p. 103) that Acceptance is not the last and final stage in the grieving process. I prefer to distinguish between "head" acceptance and "heart" acceptance. The stage of Acceptance refers to "head" acceptance; it's more cognitive in nature. We simply begin to use a language for acceptance. The last stage, though, Reorganization of Life is "heart" acceptance. This is where we move from language and thought to actual changes in our emotions and behaviors. In other words, it can take a while for the emotions to catch up to the thoughts, the result is a new way of living in relation to the past loss.

Jennifer had experienced significant healing in relation to her past rape as she worked through the cycle of grief. However, grief seems to take up residence in a tender place that can be pricked and reactivated whenever a new grieving experience comes along. This was the case for Jennifer when she discovered that her husband had been having an affair. The feeling of betrayal in her life was compounded tenfold.

The four marks of healing

I never know if a couple will survive an affair. And usually this is exactly what I say. I then go on to share that, in my experience, I have observed four marks of healing that have to be in place for the couple to have a true possibility of restoration. These marks are: (1) genuine remorse on the part of the offending spouse. That means no excuses. It also means that sorrow comes not from having been caught, but from the depths of guilt over the destructive nature of one's individual choices. (2) A willingness on the part of the offending spouse to become the receptacle for the other person's pain. Usually the offended spouse needs to repeatedly unload the anger that is part of the cycle of grief. In this case, the offending spouse needs to endure this pain supportively for as long as it takes (the sufferer needs a fellow sufferer on the way toward restoration and healing). (3) Both people need to carry their lives individually to God in prayer on a daily basis, requesting forgiveness and strength to restore the marriage. (4) The couple needs to be able to remember a time when their life together was better, a time when they enjoyed one another's company. Without this last mark of healing I rarely see a marriage survive an affair.

When I first began doing marital work with couples struggling through an affair, I only mentioned prayer as part of my concluding thoughts. Over the years, however, I have become increasingly aware of the necessity of this discipline. It is so crucial to the healing process that I admonish each couple to make it a daily practice. A true milestone in the recovery process has occurred when a couple is able pray together.

Sadly, the marriage between Jennifer and her husband did not survive. Her husband continued to confuse reasons with excuses, he refused to listen to his wife's anger, and the couple could not remember a time when their relationship was good. In addition, and perhaps most importantly, there was no commitment on the part of the husband to carry his life before God in prayer. He was attempting to do it all on his own. And this is exactly how he got into trouble in the first place.

Jennifer genuinely attempted to work at the restoration process. She didn't give up easily. However, she had learned through the grief work surrounding the childhood rape that she could not control another person's actions. Her husband, she concluded, had made his choices and would have to live with them. What she needed to do now was to establish a secure environment for herself and her children, and to move forward with life. This didn't mean that there wouldn't be any more grief work to do. To the contrary, I needed to help Jennifer move through the hinge called Depression on her way toward Acceptance and Reorganization of Life.

The Psalms As a Resource for Grieving

One of the resources that Jennifer found to be especially helpful was a reflection on the individual lament psalms from the Old Testament. The psalms were the prayers and hymns of the Old Testament Church. And in true Hebrew form, these psalms were direct, heartfelt expressions of faith.

I asked Jennifer if she was familiar with Psalm 23. She said "no" until I started to recite it, "The Lord is my shepherd, I shall not be in want" (verse 1). Immediately, she knew the psalm and was able to continue the next couple of phrases, "He makes me to lie down in green pastures . . . he restores my soul" (verses 2-3). Then I asked her if she was familiar with Psalm 22. She responded, "No, I'm sure I don't know that one. In fact, Psalm 23 is probably the only one that I'm familiar with." So I began to read from Psalm 22, "My God, my God, why have you forsaken me?" (verse 1).

Jennifer appeared puzzled, but interested to see where I was going with this discussion. I went on to explain that Psalm 23 is probably the best known psalm, in part because it "sings" with the reassuring presence of God. Psalm 22, on the other hand, speaks of the hiddenness and absence of God. What's interesting, though, is that when Jesus hung upon the cross he chose to speak the words of Psalm 22 to reflect the experience of his heart, not Psalm 23. It was as if Jesus was saying that we must go through Psalm 22 on our way toward Psalm 23. Perhaps this is a model for the restoration process in our own lives.

A Daily Dying and Rising

Jennifer and I went back to the image of the cycle of grief. I suggested that what we needed to do was place a cross right in the center of the grief experience.

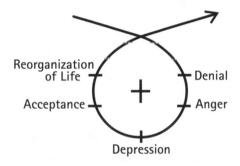

The idea of seeing the cross in the middle of the cycle of grief led us into a discussion about the sacrament of Holy Baptism. In Romans 6:4 Paul explains, "We were therefore buried with [Jesus] through baptism into death in order that, just as Christ was raised from the dead through the glory of the Father, we too may live a new life." We observed together that baptism unites us with Christ in his death and resurrection and that the cycle of grief has both a dying side and a rising side.

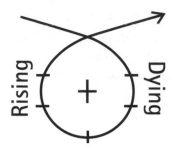

The sixteenth century Church reformer, Martin Luther, makes a daily application of the power of Holy Baptism in his Small Catechism when he writes, "It [baptism] indicates that the Old Adam in us should by daily contrition and repentance be drowned and die with all sins and evil desires, and that a new man should daily emerge and arise to live before God in righteousness and purity forever."

What a wonderful way to understand how baptism unites us to Christ. Daily we experience a dying and rising. Regularly we must go through Psalm 22 (dying) on our way toward Psalm 23 (rising). Death and resurrection have an immediate application to our lives through the cycle of grief. This is no mere psychological description. Rather, this cycle is deeply spiritual and profound. Through it we can see the cross of Christ. We can experience the marks of death and the renewal of the resurrection . . . daily.

Prayer

Risen Christ,
I die and rise daily.
My grief overwhelms and abates.
I am grateful for your strong presence.
Abide with me always.
Amen.

"Her children arise and call her blessed" is the name of this picture inspired by Proverbs 31:28. For Teri, this image represents the fruits of her long road toward spiritual restoration. Out of harshness God has brought forth tenderness, and through the fire . . . warmth.

Children run to Teri, and she embraces them. They feel safe and secure in her presence. Her own cries for help have been answered, and now she responds to the cries of others. But more than that, she instills peace and wisdom, comfort and strength.

CHAPTER TEN

THE THREE-TIERED BRAIN AND A PLACE CALLED "PLAY"

Teri, age 32

Teri was one of the most nurturing moms I have ever observed. But, as she explains, it hasn't always been that way. She had to learn how to be nurturing toward her daughter since she had not been nurtured herself.

In addition to the absence of nurture, Teri was sexually abused from the age of eleven until she was placed in foster care at the age of thirteen. Unfortunately, she was subjected to further abuse in this environment until she moved out on her own at the age of seventeen. Today, she has a daughter, age twelve, is not married, and is an assistant manager of a children's clothing store. She loves her work and enjoys being a mom. She will be the first to tell you, however, that it hasn't always been this way. "I just didn't seem to be wired to provide my daughter with the nurture that she required," Teri said. "It was as if that part of my brain was missing."

Obviously, Teri's observation about part of her brain missing isn't correct. However, she is probably closer to the truth than she realizes. In fact, Teri's story gives us an opportunity to talk about the importance of the three-tiered brain and a place called "play." Her story also provides a window into the restorative power of a caring community of faith. First, we will explore the three-tiered brain as outlined by world-renowned neuroscientist Paul MacLean of the National Institute of Mental Health.

The Three-Tiered Brain

According to Dr. MacLean, a simplistic view of the three-tiered brain would look something like this:

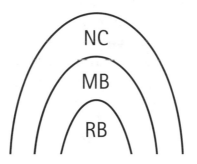

The lower part of the brain is the Reptilian Brain (RB). This is the automatic response system, the first responder in the event of an emergency. For example, if a car begins to swerve over into your lane, you don't sit and contemplate your options. Rather, you move instinctively to get out of harm's way. Such a reflex response can either take the form of fight or flight, but the key is the automatic nature of the response. In the case of some trauma events, such as childhood sexual abuse, a third type of response often occurs. This is the "freeze" mode, like a mouse that goes limp when a cat picks it up in its mouth. A child cannot fight or flee in the face of a perpetrator. The threat of power (either stated or implied) leads a child's automatic response system to shut down, go numb, and not feel.

The middle part of the brain is the Mammalian Brain (MB). This is commonly referred to as the seat of emotions, the place of nurture, comfort, and play. Within a healthy family context, this is the part of the brain that experiences a warm sense of being and presence without demands or performance expectations. I like to say that this is where we learn about the *who, when,* and *why* of life in contra-distinction to the *what* and the *how*. In other words, this is the place called play, where we learn to appreciate what makes life worth living.

The third and by far the largest part (85 percent) of the brain is what we call the Neo Cortex (NC). This is where we experience the functions of reason, abstraction, and creativity. This is also the part of the brain that has often received the most attention as can be seen by the large number of books on the distinction between right and left hemispheres.

The Mammalian Brain and Healing

It is my observation that the second tier, the Mammalian Brain, is the portion of the brain that deserves more attention as we seek to address the needs of one who has been sexually abused. This is because the feelings of protection and nurture have been largely underdeveloped, whereas the "freeze" response of the RB and the analytical-response mode (read: protective) of the NC have been overutilized. If the abused person is going to establish a sense of normalcy, there will need to be a great deal of attention given to the role of the MB.

One of the reasons why individual or group therapy holds so much promise for the abused is that they can experience a supportive, affirming, and nurturing environment within which to begin taking risks and developing trust. It has been especially interesting for me as a male therapist to see the positive responses of women who have been abused by men. The ability to develop a trusting relationship with me allows them to extend this trust toward others outside of the therapeutic relationship. By far, though, the healthiest individuals I see are those who have embarked on a spiritual journey and connected with a community of faith in significant ways. In contrast to the therapeutic relationship, the community of faith offers a type of extended-family experience that continues well beyond the bounds of traditional therapy.

When Teri expressed feeling as though a part of her brain was missing, she was really referring to the fact that the functioning of her MB was underdeveloped. She couldn't easily access her nurturing response when her daughter needed it. She always felt about one step behind where her daughter was emotionally. This had become frustrating for both Teri and her daughter. But the good news was that, through a great deal of pain and effort, Teri was able to learn how to access this part of her brain more effectively.

The MB is beginning to receive more attention by researchers, especially in the treatment of post-traumatic stress disorder. However, there seems to be a wide range of applications when it comes to understanding the role of the MB in overall brain development, healthy emotional attachment, and socialization. The underutilization of the MB seems particularly pronounced in the person who has been sexually abused during childhood. These individuals frequently demonstrate a difficulty with the concept of "play." Often these adults talk about never having experienced a childhood. They can't remember a time that seemed carefree, secure, and playful. Such concepts sound wonderful yet foreign to them. And the idea of relaxing . . . what's that? Life is too unpredictable, too unstable, too dangerous to relax. Hypervigilance is the operational standard in their life.

Faith Communities and Healing

Teri addressed her need for healing by participating in a bibliotherapy group with four other women. These women held each other accountable to read and discuss a book on recovering from childhood sexual abuse. She also came to individual therapy for about two years. In addition, she became connected to a church, a community of faith where she could gradually explore God's calling upon her life. For Teri, this calling took the form of a children's puppet ministry that she helped to establish and develop. It was truly amazing to observe how her own need for a sense of play became expressed through teaching other children about God's love in the context of play.

Certainly it would be foolish to suggest that Teri's abuse was a blessing, as evil is never a blessing. On the other hand, her story does provide an example of how God can work through the worst experiences to bring about something beautiful.

Forgiveness and the Ability to Extend Mercy and Hope

Teri is an excellent example of one who has known great injury and despair from an early age yet experienced God's work though her life to create a capacity for mercy and hope that she could extend toward others.

One of my favorite stories from the Bible is the Old Testament account of the life of Joseph, another person who was able to extend mercy and hope. You remember, the boy with the coat of many colors. His story is one of both tragedy and triumph. No sooner did he begin to enjoy great blessing in his life than he found himself in the darkest pit of despair and confusion. However, in the end Joseph, like Teri, was able to look back at his life and see the hand of God leading, guiding, protecting, and healing along the path toward spiritual maturity.

As a young boy, Joseph experienced a deeply profound sense that his father dearly loved him. His brothers, on the other hand, grew increasingly jealous and resentful toward Joseph until they plotted to sell him into slavery with a caravan headed for Egypt. They told their father that Joseph had been eaten by wild animals.

While in Egypt Joseph came to the attention of a prominent businessman named Potiphar. He took Joseph under his wing and placed him in charge of all of his land holdings. This was a significant break for Joseph who up to this time was simply grieving the loss of his home, family, and freedom. Things were definitely looking up for this young man until Potiphar's wife tried to seduce him. When Joseph resisted, Potiphar's wife lied and said that Joseph had attacked her. Potiphar had Joseph thrown into prison, the epitome of hopelessness and despair.

During his time in prison, Joseph gained the favor of the warden who placed Joseph in charge. Joseph was given the gift of interpreting dreams and was able to help a fellow prisoner interpret his dream. This man was so grateful that he promised to remember Joseph following his release and to work for Joseph's release as well. However, after the man got out of prison, he forgot about Joseph and consequently did not keep his promise. Another defeating experience.

In the course of time Pharaoh, the king of Egypt, had a dream that no one could interpret. Seeking the king's favor, the man whose dream Joseph had interpreted while in prison came to the Pharaoh and told him about Joseph. The Pharaoh called for Joseph, and he was able to interpret the dream for the king. In addition, Joseph was able to advise the king on how to prepare for the famine that the dream foretold. As his reward, the king made Joseph second in charge over the entire kingdom. Not a bad gig for a poor, young man who had been sold into slavery.

Joseph's interpretation of the king's dream came true and a great famine spread across the land. The famine even extended to Joseph's homeland of Palestine where his father and brothers were growing afraid of starvation. Joseph's father sent his sons to Egypt to request food since the Egyptians had been preparing for the famine under Joseph's instruction. And who do you think the brothers were brought to stand before and plead for food—for their very lives—but their brother Joseph. Although they did not immediately recognize him, Joseph recognized them. He asked questions about their father and whether or not they had any more brothers. At this the men became genuinely remorseful as they relayed the story of how they had mistreated one of their brothers so long ago.

Finally, Joseph couldn't hold back the truth any longer. He revealed that he was indeed their brother and they all wept and held one another. True sorrow, repentance, and now reconciliation would prevail. They were a family once again. And then, Joseph did something remarkable. He turned to his brothers and, in spiritual maturity, he said, "While what you did was evil, God used it for his good."

In other words, he used the appropriate word to describe what his brothers did to him, namely, "evil." But he also had learned to look beyond the evil and to see the hand of God at work in his life.

I like this story on a number of levels. First, this story describes the movement of ups and downs that everyone can relate to. Second, there seems to be a maturing process for Joseph in which he became increasingly aware of God's presence in his life in spite of hardships. And third, Joseph extends mercy toward his brothers in a way that transcends all of the evil they had done to him.

It's helpful to see that Joseph didn't place himself above his brothers as can be seen in the way that he wept along with them in the end. Also, it is important to note that Joseph did not minimize his brother's actions. He named what they did as "evil." Only with God's help was Joseph able to truly forgive and rejoin his family.

For our purposes in this book, we want to ask whether or not Joseph's experience has any application to the one who has experienced childhood sexual abuse, especially in relation to forgiving the abuser. Can a person so profoundly betrayed and injured come to a place of authentic forgiveness toward the perpetrator? Certainly the refrain of Scripture rings in our ears that "whoever does not forgive will not be forgiven himself." But is such forgiveness actually possible? To which we want to respond, "with God all things are possible" (Matthew 19:26).

In the story of Joseph we see something that the one who was sexually abused rarely ever experiences, namely, genuine remorse on the part of the perpetrator. If Joseph had not observed his brothers' brokenness in relation to their sin, I wonder if he would have still felt the same mercy toward them. Maybe the best an abused person can hope for is to place the perpetrator into God's hands with the understanding that God could have mercy on him. In this way the abused can attend to his own sorrow without denying God's power to forgive. Indeed, Christ died for all people, even those who abuse. But in this case, it may be all that a person can do to acknowledge that God's mercy is available even to the perpetrator who truly repents.

I never suggest that the abused needs to be able to "feel" forgiveness toward the abuser as a condition of healing. It is enough simply to acknowledge that the abuser is in God's hands and that God will determine what to do . . . even if this means that God will forgive the abuser.

Teri is a person who has experienced God's grace and tender healing touch. And, like Joseph, she seeks to regularly demonstrate this toward the children and parents she ministers to. It is not possible to spend even five minutes in Teri's presence and not feel that you have been in the presence of God. She radiates play, mercy, and hope.

Prayer

Gracious God,
Thank you for this beautiful world.
Thank you for my body and my brain and the joy
*   of play.*
Thank you for my faith community.
Thank you for calling me to you.
Amen.

A water-pool reflection is one of the simplest images of life. Yet, how often do we take the time to look at ourselves in a deep and concentrated way? As with the picture here, even looking at one small part of oneself such as a hand or foot (or thought or emotion) is a necessary first step. We don't just jump in head-to-toe and become immersed in a bath of self-disclosure. That would be too much. We might drown. But take the hand and dip the tip of it into the water and, in time, we might feel safe enough to wade in more fully.

Roger started out slowly. And I needed to be careful not to let him drown in his own vulnerability. He was a competent man with many gifts and abilities to be shared. He wasn't ready to acknowledge God's hand at work in his life, but he had begun to feel a hopefulness that could eventually open his eyes to see mercy and grace. Thankfully, Roger stopped at the water's edge just long enough to take a fresh look.

CHAPTER ELEVEN

AN ABUSE OF POWER

Roger, age 39

I have saved Roger for last because the form of abuse that he experienced is unique in that the perpetrator was a Catholic priest. All Roger wanted as a young boy was for a trusted adult male to befriend him. He lived in a home full of alcoholism and verbal and physical abuse. Surely he was afraid of risking a relationship with a male authority figure. However, his priest was the most logical place to find comfort, strength, and protection. Safety with him would never be an issue . . . or would it?

Roger remembers his priest befriending him and asking him to help him with odd jobs around the church. At first Roger felt reassured and energized by this relationship. The priest praised Roger for all of his selfless efforts. This praise helped to bolster Roger's confidence in himself. Then came the subtle, seemingly innocent arm on a shoulder and friendly pat on the rear. This latter form of touch made Roger feel a little uncomfortable, but he shrugged it off as a playful gesture. "After all," he told himself, "athletes do this all the time." What Roger didn't realize was that his defenses were being broken down a little at a time.

Finally, Roger was invited by the priest to a camp retreat with several other boys. Roger was flattered that he had been chosen to attend and he gladly accepted. But Roger would never feel the same about himself or the church after this event. During one evening after everyone had gone to bed, the priest invited Roger to join him in his room for an "important conversation." The priest told him how special he was to him and that he loved him. He told him that God loved him and had a special plan for his life. Then the priest moved closer and suggested they both take off their clothes "just for fun." Then he fondled Roger's genitals and told him to do the same to him. Roger knew instinctively that what was happening was wrong, but the priest warned him not to tell anyone and that it was all a part of being close friends. Anyway, who would believe him? He certainly couldn't expect to receive any support from his parents.

This activity continued on a weekly basis for about a year, with increasingly more devastating types of sexual interactions. Roger was eleven when all of this happened. At age thirty-nine he sat before me and it was the first time that he had ever breathed a word about it to anyone.

Roger became an alcoholic as a way to mask his depression, so the first thing he needed to do was to get sober and begin taking an antidepressant. In addition, he needed to address the abuse from both his father and the priest. There was a lot to deal with and Roger had been running from his problems for a long time. The fact that he sat with me, another man, in a private room was a huge achievement in and of itself. I was proud of him for just showing up each week.

Dealing with Anger and Rage

Roger had a difficult time accessing any emotions other than anger, and this easily turned into rage at the slightest provocation. I asked Roger to keep a daily anger journal to help him record and track the cognitive processes of his anger. Whenever he experienced rage or "out-of-control" anger he was to write down four parts to the incident. The first part is the event itself, the second is his interpretation of the event, the third is the accompanying emotions, and the fourth is his action based upon those emotions.

The next week Roger came back with several entries in his anger journal. This is an example:

Event: *The gas station attendant was slow in helping me get checked out.*

Interpretation: *The attendant was attempting to make my life difficult by taking so long. The attendant didn't want to help me because he didn't like me.*

Emotions: *Frustration, anger, rage, out-of-control.*

Action: *I yelled at the attendant and drove off fast almost hitting another car as I pulled out into traffic.*

One of the things that I ask a person to pay close attention to is the interpretation part of the journal entry. Often I find that we move so quickly in our daily experiences from events and emotions to actions that we don't easily clarify our actual interpretations of the events. Retracing our steps through the cognitive process often casts a new light on how we view ourselves. For example, if Roger would have considered a different interpretation of the event, such as the attendant was new and a little slow, he still might have felt frustrated, but probably not to the point of anger, rage, and out-of-control behaviors. The fact is, he didn't really know why the attendant was slow and to automatically assume that the attendant didn't like him and wanted to make his life difficult was a very big leap. Such an interpretation said more about how Roger viewed himself than anything else.

When I asked Roger what was the core belief about himself as demonstrated by this example, he said, "I am not a likable person and people only want to hurt me." Bingo. Now we're getting to the heart of the matter. Roger needed to restructure a more accurate, healthier view of himself. But of course this is easier said than done. The hopeful part of his story, at this point, was that he had begun to access the core beliefs that had set him up for failure in relationships. After practicing this journaling exercise for a few months, Roger began to externalize his experiences of anger while they were happening. He even learned how to anticipate his interpretations of an event as it occurred and to offer himself some alternative interpretations. This had a general calming effect and left Roger feeling more in control emotionally.

Conquering Internal Fear

In a relatively short time Roger had noticeably fewer journal entries to share each week. "I just don't seem to get angry as often," he said with a smile. The combination of the antidepressant and the cognitive therapy was more effective than either would have been alone.

Roger was encouraged about his external relationships, but he now turned our attention to his internal world. He had awful, recurring nightmares that left him drenched in sweat and shaking when he awoke in the morning. The nightmares had been with him for several years, but lately the frequency had increased.

Roger recounted the nightmare:

I'm in a dark room with a man dressed in black. He is coming toward me slowly. I know he wants to hurt me so I turn to the door, but the door is locked from the outside. I can't open it. I try and try and try. I attempt to yell out but my voice is constricted and I can barely muster a whisper. Anyway, no one hears me. The man is moving very slowly toward me. It's as though he knows that he has all the time in the world. But with each step that he takes I become more terrified. Finally, I wake up shaking and drenched in sweat. I'm afraid to go back to sleep.

Roger was visibly shaken as he recounted this dream. His pupils dilated, respiration increased, skin became pale, sweating increased, and he complained of feeling cold. He thought he was going to be sick. Obviously the dream amounted to a reenactment, a retraumatization of the childhood sexual abuse. Roger was not a small man. He was a medium-sized man with a physical strength that testified to the fact that he worked as a landscaper. However, this childhood trauma had a way of quickly reducing him to a helpless state. "I just can't seem to get rid of these thoughts," explained Roger. "I feel that I should be able to conquer these old fears, but I can't shake it."

We decided to take a break from the dream and come back to it the next week. Roger needed a chance to regulate his physical and emotional states before proceeding. I explained that during the next session we would take a closer look at the elements of this recurring dream and decipher what the dream is calling Roger to focus on. I instructed Roger to simply write down any random thoughts that came to mind associated with the dream during the week.

At our next session, Roger shared the following thoughts that he had written down about his dream: "Darkness, black, sin, demonic, terrifying, loss of control, immobilizing, overpowering, helpless, fighting for survival, alone." I asked Roger if he saw anything in this list that seemed hopeful. He said, "At least I'm fighting to survive." Exactly.

Roger explained that the meaning of the dream to him was obvious. "I was in a room with a priest and couldn't escape his abuse. Although," he went on, "the door was never locked. In real life I could have gotten up and walked out. I guess that I was so frightened and confused as a child that I felt trapped. The priest wasn't even a large man. But his authority, his position as a priest overpowered me. I had been taught to respect him and that he only ever intended me good."

Today I sat in the presence of a giant. Roger was more than a survivor. He was becoming a thriver. He was learning how to transcend his past and to develop a language to describe his experiences. He was no longer getting stuck in his emotional responses, but was beginning to gain more control. And I was very proud of him and his willingness to work so hard at the healing process.

Coming into Relationship with God

Several times throughout the course of my discussions with Roger I attempted to talk about God. However, he had so closely tied a relationship with God to the institutional church that he couldn't separate the two. And since his experiences with the institutional church had resulted in such misery, he was rarely open to talking about God. He would say, "I can see that this is important to you, and I respect that. But God just doesn't work for me." And then I reminded myself that Roger had sought me out, a pastoral counselor. And Roger kept showing up to talk with me week after week. Perhaps I needed to be thankful for the fact that Roger might have the opportunity to learn about God's love through me even if I never get to see him make this connection during my time with him.

I love the reflecting pool image at the beginning of this chapter because it seems to portray an important aspect of our relationship with God. We don't always jump into this relationship all at once. We test the waters to see what happens. We want to find out if "God works." Over time we learn to trust—but only gradually—until we grow in our ability to linger in the presence of God and see this as a safe place to be. At this point, we can begin to see the hand of God inviting us. For Roger, he had gone from touching the pool of water with his finger to stepping in and getting wet all the way up to his knees.

A child's perspective of people and environments is influenced by their own small size and their experience. I remember, for example, going back to visit the first house that I grew up in and being amazed at how small the house was. As a child the house seemed huge. But it wasn't. In fact, by most standards, the house was pretty small. The point is that I didn't experience the house as small when I was a child.

Adults have an automatic responsibility to look out for the well-being of the children in their care. Children cannot be expected to understand all of their limitations and the inherent dangers of their environment. A person in a professional role, whether a medical doctor, counselor, or clergyperson, must take full responsibility to establish the rules and boundaries for relationships to ensure the safety of everyone concerned. This is especially true when children are involved.

Over time Roger was able to make an important distinction between the way he experienced a priest as a child and as an adult. The role of priest carries a lot of weight since religious leaders are often equated with God in the eyes of children. Even at age eleven, Roger perceived the priest and God to definitely be on the same team. Whatever the priest said was tantamount to hearing the voice of God. Even if the priest abused his powers, as in this case, Roger had been taught to automatically assume the best about the priest. It was unthinkable that he (and God) would ever intend him harm.

When a professional such as a priest betrays a child's trust, it makes sense that the rebuilding process for trust will be a slow one. A consistent, positive lingering in the presence of a "God-person" like a priest or other clergy can help the one so betrayed to learn that God is trustworthy. Time and a caring presence are the essential ingredients.

Prayer

God,
I do not know how to trust you.
I do know if I want to trust you.
Help me wade into the water.
Amen.

PART THREE

FINAL THOUGHTS

CHAPTER TWELVE

SUFFERING AND
YOUR RELATIONSHIP
WITH GOD

Throughout this book I have attempted to let each individual speak for him- or herself. The effects of childhood sexual abuse appear in various forms and degrees. No two people are exactly alike. Consequently, it is not possible to take a "one-size-fits-all" approach to the healing process. There are, however, a number of consistent elements in my journey with folks who have been abused. One of these is the question of how a God who is supposedly good and all-powerful could have allowed such crimes to occur in the life of a helpless child. And I think this is a fair and honest question that needs to be addressed if a person is going to make real headway in the spiritual restoration process. This chapter is devoted to the question of suffering and your relationship with God.

Examining Suffering on Three Levels

In classic literature, we call the question of evil and suffering in the world a "theodicy." Theodicy comes from two Greek words, *theos* and *dike,* which mean "God" and "justice" respectively. In other words, this is the "Just-God" question: "Is God truly a Just God?" or "If God is Good and All-Powerful, then how could God allow suffering and abuse in the world?"

I want to suggest that it is helpful to discuss the question of suffering on three different levels. The first level is the *Intellectual Level,* the second is the *Historical Level,* and the third is the *Personal Level.* My hope as we review this subject is that you may discover a language for understanding your relationship with God in the face of suffering in this world. My desire is not to defend God or to take God off the hook, but simply to provide a framework for viewing the world with all of its brokenness and pain.

The intellectual level

The intellectual level of suffering is the most detached level in which we simply seek to formulate the right questions. We listen to others who have asked questions before us, and we look for clues to find common ground. For example, we hear the individual psalms of lament in the Old Testament and conclude that there is a historical precedent for people of faith to question God and his will.

Psalm 13:1-2
How long, O Lord? Will you forget me forever?
    How long will you hide your face from me?
How long must I wrestle with my thoughts
    and every day have sorrow in my heart?
    How long will my enemy triumph over me?

Psalm 22:1-2
My God, my God, why have you forsaken me?
    Why are you so far from saving me,
    so far from the words of my groaning?
O my God, I cry out by day, but you do not answer,
    by night, and am not silent.

Psalm 44:23-24
Awake, O Lord! Why do you sleep?
    Rouse yourself! Do not reject us forever.
Why do you hide your face
    and forget our misery and oppression?

These are only a few of the many individual laments in the Bible that express the common questions of those who suffer. The basic belief is that the presence of suffering suggests the absence of God. If God were present, God would surely do something to help. In fact, the psalmist appears to go so far as to suggest that since God is not intervening to help, he is responsible for the suffering.

Throughout history, the question has been asked: "How can God be both good and all-powerful at the same time?" The rationale is that these two characteristics are mutually exclusive in the face of suffering in this world. Let me explain.

In the face of human suffering, it would be easier to accept a God who is either good or all-powerful, but not both good and all-powerful at the same time. We could accept a God who is good and who really wants to do something to help us, but is simply not powerful enough to help. Or we could accept a God who is all-powerful but not good, because if he was good he would surely use his power to help us. In this case we would conclude, then, that God must be evil.

The Bible, however, describes God as both good and all-powerful at the same time. But our view of God's two-fold character is limited by the fact that we only see God in his purest form in the first two chapters of the Bible. In Genesis 1 and 2 we gain a glimpse of God according to his true character and will for the creation.

God's original creation was a perfect world without brokenness, destruction, disease, despair, or death. This is the way God set it up. This is what God intended. No heartache, no conflict between man and woman, nature or God. Harmony, peace, security, comfort, and the feeling of God's constant presence and provision were all in place. That is, until man and woman rebelled against God. Then everything changed. And we've only made it to the third chapter of Genesis.

From chapter 3 on, we see a very different world from the one God originally created and intended. With man and woman's rebellion, the world became broken, fallen, dysfunctional, diseased, and subject to decay and death. From this point on, we have a hard time seeing the dual nature of God as both good and all-powerful because the world in its fallen state is such a mess. Could God reverse the chaos? Yes. Does God? Not for a time. Will God eventually reverse the chaos? Thoughts about that will come later in this discussion. For now, we live in a world very different from the one that God originally created. We live in a world that no longer reflects God's pure goodness and all-powerfulness. And each successive generation has to shoulder the responsibility for the brokenness of this world.

Every person is fallen and imperfect. If you follow the life of any person long enough, he or she will eventually disappoint you. For example, the Bible records that the first sibling rivalry in human history resulted in Cain killing his brother Abel. If we study the life of Noah, we are amazed at his faith in God. But after the ark rested on dry land, Noah grew a vineyard, made wine, got drunk, and made a naked fool of himself, shaming his family. And what about Abraham? Father Abraham was a pillar of faith. But when he doubted that God would keep his promise to give him a son by Sarah, he took matters into his own hands and had a son by a concubine named Hagar. Remember David? He was a great warrior, songwriter, and king—a man after God's own heart. But one day David spotted a married woman named Bathsheba and committed adultery with her. He even had her husband murdered so that he could cover up his crime. And so it goes, throughout all of Scripture. Fast forward to the New Testament and look at Peter,

James, and John. "Who among us will be the greatest in the kingdom?" they asked. What an ego trip! Yes, everyone, if you stay with them long enough, will disappoint you. And we often wonder where God is in all of this mess.

Now that we have begun asking the right questions and can see the difference between what God originally intended and the way things actually are, we can move on to the historical level of suffering.

The historical level

The historical level of suffering brings us a little closer to the personal struggle each of us has with pain. To understand the historical level we will examine the person of Job. While you may not be familiar with the story of Job, his reputation certainly precedes him. Expressions like "the patience of Job" and "the suffering of Job" have their origin in this man's story. And I can't think of a better place to start this discussion than the first two chapters of Job, a behind-the-scenes look at what led up to this man's suffering. In fact, I will include significant portions of the text (all of chapter 1 and most of chapter 2) to establish the context for our focus on the historical level of suffering.

Prologue, Job 1:1-5
In the land of Uz there lived a man whose name was Job. This man was blameless and upright; he feared God and shunned evil. He had seven sons and three daughters, and he owned seven thousand sheep, three thousand camels, five hundred yoke of oxen and five hundred donkeys, and had a large number of servants. He was the greatest man among all the people of the East. His sons used to

take turns holding feasts in their homes, and they would invite their three sisters to eat and drink with them. When a period of feasting had run its course, Job would send and have them purified. Early in the morning he would sacrifice a burnt offering for each of them, thinking, "Perhaps my children have sinned and cursed God in their hearts." This was Job's regular custom.

Job's First Test, Job 1:6-22
One day the angels came to present themselves before the Lord, and Satan also came with them. The Lord said to Satan, "Where have you come from?" Satan answered the Lord, "From roaming through the earth and going back and forth in it." Then the Lord said to Satan, "Have you considered my servant Job? There is no one on earth like him; he is blameless and upright, a man who fears God and shuns evil." "Does Job fear God for nothing?" Satan replied. "Have you not put a hedge around him and his household and everything he has? You have blessed the work of his hands, so that his flocks and herds are spread throughout the land. But stretch out your hand and strike everything he has, and he will surely curse you to your face." The Lord said to Satan, "Very well, then, everything he has is in your hands, but on the man himself do not lay a finger." Then Satan went out from the presence of the Lord.

Job was a good man who "feared God and shunned evil." He was also a wealthy man and enjoyed a prosperous life with his wife and ten children. Life seemed to be going great until Satan came into the picture. Let's read what happened next.

Job 1:13-22

One day when Job's sons and daughters were feasting and drinking wine at the oldest brother's house, a messenger came to Job and said, "The oxen were plowing and the donkeys were grazing nearby, and the Sabeans attacked and carried them off. They put the servants to the sword, and I am the only one who has escaped to tell you!" While he was still speaking, another messenger came and said, "The fire of God fell from the sky and burned up the sheep and the servants, and I am the only one who has escaped to tell you!" While he was still speaking, another messenger came and said, "The Chaldeans formed three raiding parties and swept down on your camels and carried them off. They put the servants to the sword, and I am the only one who has escaped to tell you!" While he was still speaking, yet another messenger came and said, "Your sons and daughters were feasting and drinking wine at the oldest brother's house, when suddenly a mighty wind swept in from the desert and struck the four corners of the house. It collapsed on them and they are dead, and I am the only one who has escaped to tell you!" At this, Job got up and tore his robe and shaved his head. Then he fell to the ground in worship and said:

"Naked I came from my mother's womb,
and naked I will depart.
The Lord gave and the Lord has taken away;
may the name of the Lord be praised."

In all this, Job did not sin by charging God with wrongdoing.

Job is truly an amazing man of faith. He lost everything that he had worked so hard for, his children were all killed in a tornado, and he still maintains that God is not to blame. Surely he has suffered enough, even more than his share. What more could possibly happen to this man?

Job's Second Test Job 2:1-10
On another day the angels came to present themselves before the Lord, and Satan also came with them to present himself before him. And the Lord said to Satan, "Where have you come from?" Satan answered the Lord, "From roaming through the earth and going back and forth in it." Then the Lord said to Satan, "Have you considered my servant Job? There is no one on earth like him; he is blameless and upright, a man who fears God and shuns evil. And he still maintains his integrity, though you incited me against him to ruin him without any reason." "Skin for skin!" Satan replied. "A man will give all he has for his own life. But stretch out your hand and strike his flesh and bones, and he will surely curse you to your face." The Lord said to Satan, "Very well, then, he is in your hands; but you must spare his life." So Satan went out from the presence of the Lord and afflicted Job with painful sores from the soles of his feet to the top of his head. Then Job took a piece of broken pottery and scraped himself with it as he sat among the ashes. His wife said to him, "Are you still holding on to your integrity? Curse God and die!" He replied,

"You are talking like a foolish woman. Shall we accept good from God, and not trouble?" In all this, Job did not sin in what he said.

Now we've seen everything. This is more suffering than most of us will ever endure. And still Job does not charge God with wrongdoing. Maybe he should. After all, God allowed Satan to test Job. Obviously, God had the ultimate say as can be seen in the fact that God placed Job "into the hands" of Satan. Satan could only go as far as God allowed. So why not follow his wife's suggestion to "curse God and die" (Job 2:9)?

I have to admit that this story deeply troubles me. I don't like to imagine that God could be playing a game at Job's expense. It's not too difficult to move from this historical account of suffering to my own life and imagine that if God could do this to Job, God could also do this to me. And what about this man Job? How could he not break down and at least question God in the middle of his misery? Job seems almost too good to be true.

Fortunately, we don't have to wait very long before we see a side of Job that we can more easily relate to. By chapter 3, Job begins to question God and God's wisdom.

Job 3:1-8
After this, Job opened his mouth and cursed the day of his birth. He said: "May the day of my birth perish, and the night it was said, 'A boy is born!' That day—may it turn to darkness; may God above not care about it; may no light shine upon it. May darkness and deep shadow claim it once more; may a cloud settle over it; may blackness overwhelm its light. That night—may thick darkness seize it; may

it not be included among the days of the year nor be entered in any of the months. May that night be barren; may no shout of joy be heard in it. May those who curse days curse that day.

Job wishes that he had never been born. Why would God allow him to see the light of day if this great suffering was to be the end result? What good purpose could Job's destruction serve? Job's complaints grow stronger by chapter ten.

Job 10:1-9
"I loathe my very life; therefore I will give free rein to my complaint and speak out in the bitterness of my soul. I will say to God: Do not condemn me, but tell me what charges you have against me. Does it please you to oppress me, to spurn the work of your hands, while you smile on the schemes of the wicked? Do you have eyes of flesh? Do you see as a mortal sees? Are your days like those of a mortal or your years like those of a man, that you must search out my faults and probe after my sin—though you know that I am not guilty and that no one can rescue me from your hand? Your hands shaped me and made me. Will you now turn and destroy me? Remember that you molded me like clay. Will you now turn me to dust again?

Obviously Job was a finite human being who honestly questioned the wisdom of God. Certainly, we can understand his need to do so. Such questioning doesn't mean that Job was without faith. In fact, he addressed his questions directly to God, trusting that God was big enough to handle whatever he threw God's way. And the story (and suffering) continues on for forty-two chapters. When will there be relief for this man? What can we possibly learn about the role of suffering as we look at Job's life along with other people who suffered in the Bible? These are important questions for us to ask.

The Three Roles of Suffering

I would like to suggest that, for the person of faith, there are at least three roles that suffering can play in our lives. First, suffering can be *a punishment for sin*. Second, suffering can act as *a barrier to sin*. And third, suffering can be used *to bring glory to God and point us to Christ* in whom we have our ultimate hope.

A punishment for sin

Suffering as a punishment for sin is probably the first place that most of us go to answer the question of suffering in our lives. We simply conclude that we (or others) must have done something to deserve this affliction or heartache. And we're not alone in thinking this way. You may remember that Job had three friends who tried to counsel him in his distress. The bottom line of their counsel was this: "Job. You must have sin in your life for which you have not repented. Come clean. Get it out in the open. Fess up. And God will have mercy on you and take away your punishment." Simple enough. But the truth is that Job was fully transparent before God. He prayed regularly, offered sacrifices for sins, and received God's forgiveness on a daily basis. And he knew it. While suffering certainly can be a punishment for sin, Job was clear that there had to be another explanation for his suffering.

How are we to understand suffering as punishment for sin in our everyday lives? Perhaps a few examples will help us think about it. If we choose to smoke when we know it is destroying our lungs, our choice brings us suffering. When we are abusive to others, our choice brings brokenness and suffering into our relationships. I do not believe, nor did Job, that God directly inflicts punishment. Rather, each choice we make in our freedom from God can work for good or evil in the world. Our choices and the choices of others can bring healing or suffering.

Victims of childhood sexual abuse are not suffering because God is punishing them for a sin. Rather, suffering is in their life because of someone else's choices, someone else's broken relationship with themselves and with God. God's desire is that you be healed from this suffering and to that end God continually invites you into a relationship.

A barrier to sin

Suffering as a barrier to sin is what I liken to a "fire-line." A fire-line is one of the tools that firefighters use to fight a forest fire. They burn a line ahead of the raging fire so that when the forest fire reaches the burn line there is no more fuel to keep it alive and it burns itself out. Similarly the role of suffering can work as a barrier to sin.

St. Paul understood this concept as well as anyone. Paul described his personal affliction as a "thorn in the flesh." We don't know what this "thorn" was exactly, but we do know that it caused him great pain. We also know that Paul prayed for God to take this affliction away from him. Over and over again he prayed. And God said, "No." The explanation that Paul gives for why God allowed this suffering was to keep him humble and to always remind him that God's grace is sufficient for all of his needs. In other words, God allowed suffering in Paul's life to act as a fire-line or barrier so that pride would not rage out of control.

And so it is with our lives as well. We often express a greater need for God in the midst of our weakness and troubles. Just when we think we have figured out the secret to a successful life or have made it to a financially "safe" place or have our children on the right track, the bottom seems to fall out. At this point we can choose one of two paths. Either we can turn away from God or we can recognize our great need for God. It's this latter choice that will lead us into a closer relationship with God. And our personal sense of success will be tempered with the renewed appreciation that we are completely dependent upon God for everything once again.

With respect to our friend Job, however, this barrier-to-sin function of suffering still isn't a satisfactory explanation. God described Job as a good and just man who regularly worshiped him with his whole life. There was no need for a fire-line role of suffering in Job's life. Besides, we already know that Job's suffering was a direct result of Satan's challenge to God (or was that God's challenge to Satan?).

To bring glory to God and to point us to Christ

Suffering as a means to bring glory to God and to point us to Christ is the third use or role that we want to consider. And there is a great story in the New Testament about a man born blind who helps us see this role more clearly.

Jesus Heals a Man Born Blind

John 9:1-11
As [Jesus] went along, he saw a man blind from birth. His disciples asked him, "Rabbi, who sinned,

this man or his parents, that he was born blind?" "Neither this man nor his parents sinned," said Jesus, "but this happened so that the work of God might be displayed in his life. As long as it is day, we must do the work of him who sent me. Night is coming, when no one can work. While I am in the world, I am the light of the world." Having said this, he spit on the ground, made some mud with the saliva, and put it on the man's eyes. "Go," he told him, "wash in the Pool of Siloam" (this word means Sent). So the man went and washed, and came home seeing. His neighbors and those who had formerly seen him begging asked, "Isn't this the same man who used to sit and beg?" Some claimed that he was. Others said, "No, he only looks like him." But he himself insisted, "I am the man." "How then were your eyes opened?" they demanded. He replied, "The man they call Jesus made some mud and put it on my eyes. He told me to go to Siloam and wash. So I went and washed, and then I could see."

In this story we find a man who was blind from birth. The disciples asked the question, "Who sinned?" In other words, they were operating with the same limited view of suffering that Job's friends had. They believed that suffering must be a direct punishment for sin. Jesus, however, was quick to explain that the blindness was not a punishment for sin, rather it existed "so that the work of God might be displayed in his life." Jesus showed forth the glory of God by healing the man and also pointed to himself as the promised Savior. This was the purpose and role of suffering in this man's life. "'How were your eyes opened?' the people demanded. He replied, 'The man they call Jesus.'" This is where we end up in the story, with the man they call Jesus. He is the healer. He is the great physician. He is the one about whom we sing in the great old spiritual "Amazing Grace," singing, "I once was blind but now I see."

This third purpose and role of suffering is the one that comes closest to our understanding of what happened to Job. This was an opportunity for God to show forth God's grace, mercy, and restorative power. This was an opportunity for God to point Job, his friends, and all who hear the story to the one who originates and sustains life, namely, God. In fact, the very middle of Job's story is where we find one of the greatest resurrection passages of all time. If you take the story of Job (forty-two chapters) and divide it in two, you will come pretty close to 19:25-27, which reads as follows:

> I know that my Redeemer lives, and that in the end *(when Christ returns at the end of time)* he will stand upon the earth. And after my skin has been destroyed *(death)*, yet in my flesh will I see God *(resurrection)*; I myself will see him with my own eyes—I, and not another. How my heart yearns within me! (my comments added in parentheses)

This is truly amazing. Right in the middle of Job's story, in the middle of his life, in the middle of his misery, God gave him (and us) one of the greatest visions of hope that we could ever receive. This is the hope of the resurrection. This is the heart of Handel's *Messiah*. This is a picture of restoration and final victory over Satan, sin, and death. Job can see the ultimate outcome of his faith. It's not this suffering after all. But suffering must come first.

No one understands suffering like one who has suffered. And no one can comfort another like one who has known comfort. There's a great passage from 2 Corinthians in which Paul speaks to this very issue. Paul says,

> Praise be to the God and Father of our Lord Jesus Christ, the Father of compassion and the God of all comfort, who comforts us in all our troubles, *so that we can comfort those in any trouble with the comfort we ourselves have received from God* (2 Corinthians 1:3-4, emphasis added).

In other words, when we receive comfort from God for our afflictions, we then have the opportunity to share this comfort with others and thereby let them know from whom this comfort ultimately comes. In fact, when we read further in Paul's letter, we see this very connection made to the sufferings of Christ.

> For just as the sufferings of Christ flow over into our lives, so also through Christ our comfort overflows. If we are distressed, it is for your comfort and salvation; if we are comforted, it is for your comfort, which produces in you patient endurance of the same sufferings we suffer (2 Corinthians 1:5-6).

The Personal Level of Suffering

We are now ready to move on to the personal level of suffering with a focus on Jesus and how our lives intersect with his life. Job was speaking about this Jesus in Job 19: 25-27. In the life, death, and resurrection of Jesus we find our greatest comfort and consolation in the midst of our own hardships in life.

Jesus, you will remember, wasn't always human. Our Christian tradition confesses that the Son existed from eternity together with the Father and the Holy Spirit. Jesus was removed from all human suffering until God decided to take on human flesh as a babe in Bethlehem. This was a truly remarkable decision on the part of God because from this point on the second person of the Holy Trinity was both fully God and fully human. This God-man, Jesus, would forever have a dual-nature. And this is radically important for you and me.

In the person of Jesus, God came to us and became one of us. Oh, Jesus continued to be fully divine. But because he was also fully human, he could experience life as we experience it. He could, in the end, stand before us with credibility and say, "I understand what you are going through, not just intellectually, but experientially as well." He was tempted as we are tempted. He experienced hunger and thirst. He knew the devastation of losing loved ones, first with the beheading of his cousin and friend, John the Baptist, and then with the death of his friend Lazarus at whose tomb he wept. Jesus understood the need for companionship as he gathered his disciples around him. He also felt the deep pains of betrayal, first by Judas, then by the rest of his disciples. And finally, Jesus experienced the torturous and shameful death by crucifixion. It is here, at the cross, where we want to dwell for a time of reflection.

Jesus chose his last words carefully as he hung upon the cross. Perhaps most striking is the sense of outrage that he felt as he cried out the words of Psalm 22 in despair, saying, "My God, my God, why have you forsaken me?" Somehow Jesus knew *in the core of his being* that what he was experiencing was not of God. Somehow he knew that this suffering flew in the face of everything that God had originally intended for his creation. Jesus was experiencing our brokenness, our fallenness, our desperation, and our death. And Jesus experienced our question "Why?"

The question "Why?" is *our* question, for we know *in the core of our being* that the world in which we live is very different from the one that God originally intended. We see people hungry, and we know that's not right. We see people naked, and we know that's not okay. We watch as family members and friends have their bodies ravished by disease, and we feel outraged as we cry out the question, "Why?" But where do we go from here? What are the options once we ask the question "Why?"

As Jesus hung upon the cross, he had two options for his outrage. He could remain stuck in the question "Why?" and thereby adopt a nihilistic, despairing view of life that says existence is senseless and useless. This is the viewpoint of radical, terrorist groups. This is the basis for committing suicide. Or Jesus could find a way to move past the question "Why?"

Henri Nouwen tells the story of his conversation with two friends who were trapeze artists. One was the flyer and the other the catcher. His question was mainly for the flyer. He asked, "What do you do to make sure that you will be caught?" The response by his friend was instructive. He said, "I simply let go, remain still, and trust that I will be caught at the right time." And in a way, this is how Jesus moved beyond the question "Why?" as he hung upon the cross. For this question was not his last word. His last word was to say, "Father, into your hands I commit my spirit." Then, the gospel writer tells us, he breathed his last. In other words, Jesus let go of the bar, remained still, and trusted that he would be caught "at the right time."

Thankfully, Jesus did not remain bound by the grave. As he had foretold (and as Job had already seen in Job 19:25), Jesus rose from the dead on the third day. In his resurrection, Jesus proclaimed ultimate victory over Satan, sin, and death. Jesus took his outrage toward the sin and destruction of this fallen world and demonstrated his desire to restore his creation, first in his own body and finally for all at the end of time. On the last day when Jesus returns in glory, he will restore his creation back to the way he originally intended it to be. No more hunger or thirst. No more abandonment or abuse. No more disease or pain. No more tears or death.

This final resurrection is our ultimate hope. But even now, on this side of heaven in the midst of our tears and pain, Jesus invites us to ask the question "Why?" and in so doing calls us to an outrage that seeks restoration and renewal. He wants us to feed the hungry, clothe the naked, protect the most vulnerable, and fund research for diseases. He wants us to fight against the ravages and deceit of Satan's voice. He wants us to let go of our own selfish and destructive ways, to listen carefully to the still small voice of the Spirit, and to trust that God will catch us "at the right time." For now we fight. For now we take up a healthy rebellion, a countercultural stance, and a role of advocacy for those too helpless to defend themselves. In other words, we remain in this strange tension between resting and fighting until our Lord returns to take us to heaven.

This whole discussion about the experience and role of suffering in our lives has multiple applications for those who have been the victims of abuse. The feelings of outrage and abandonment that result in the question "Why?" provide a significant connection to Jesus as he hung upon the cross. Likewise, the victim of abuse can identify with the need to look beyond the question "Why?" and see an opportunity to bring God glory and point others to restoration in Jesus.

There is never anything good about abuse. It's not what God originally intended. God rightfully receives our question "Why?" It's this question that marks us as a child of God, a person of faith, who knows *in the core of his or her being* that something terrible has gone wrong with God's world. The outrage and rebellion against sin are honest and necessary responses. And we pray that God will enable us to use this energy and the force of our anger to protect and preserve the most vulnerable of this world. The victim of abuse wants to end up where Jesus did, rested and assured in the arms of God, where they can protect and care for those who can't speak for themselves.

Conclusion

I hope that these thoughts on suffering and your relationship to God challenge you to see the world from a different perspective. I hope these thoughts help you discover that Jesus is much closer to you than you may have realized. I hope that you find that your outrage and anger toward abuse are sacred feelings and an important part of your experience with God.

Throughout this book we have had the privilege of walking alongside of those who have suffered various forms and degrees of sexual abuse as children. I have not attempted to address the experiences of the adult who has been sexually abused during adulthood (rape, etc.) nor have I written this book for children who have been the victim of abuse, though many aspects of the healing process apply to each of these cases as well. My focus, rather, has been on the adult who, many years after the initial childhood abuse, struggles to find peace and relational satisfaction in his or her life. Adult victims of childhood sexual abuse are capable people, successful people, and people I would readily turn to for help and guidance in my own life. They are also people who often carry with them an intense feeling of shame that can overwhelm them in a secret place of suffering.

The parable of Lazarus and the Rich Man in chapter 7 provided an outline of the spiritual restoration process in three stages, namely, Pre-Death, Death, and New Life. Hopefully you were able to see how each person in the book was at a different place in this process. The Pre-Death and Death stages were represented by those who appeared before the chapter on Lazarus and the Rich Man, while the stage of New Life was represented by those appearing after the parable.

There is no uniformity in the way people experience the effects of abuse or its recovery. There are, however, some "marks" that help us identify movement through the three broad categories of Pre-Death, Death, and New Life. It's not that a person stops feeling a sense of outrage or disgust toward the abuse, but that these feelings become more manageable, less debilitating, and directed toward the true object of evil. In other words, there is a movement away from the feeling of being a victim toward more of a feeling of being a survivor and, even more, a thriver.

I cannot emphasize enough the importance of community in the healing process. This often occurs gradually as a person who has been victimized learns to connect with at least one other person. This can be a professional counselor or a close friend, but it must be in a safe place where there is accountability for the relationship. Eventually, the person needs to begin participating in a group setting where vulnerability and intimacy can increase over time. This can be a service group or a growth group. It doesn't really matter as long as there is an increasing experience of mutual investment in one another. Finally, a person learns how to devote himself or herself to the betterment of others while maintaining a clear sense of boundary that is guided by self-worth instead of shame. And if a person is really fortunate, she or he will begin to feel the warmth of God's presence along with a sustaining peace in her or his heart and mind. This is the spiritual restoration side of healing and wholeness. This is the place where one begins to see glimpses of ultimate hope in the resurrection of Jesus. This is the place where New Life takes on eternal dimensions, even now.

God's blessings to you as you travel the journey of faith, and as you travel with others in their journey of faith as well.

Other Resources from Augsburg

I Love You, Son by Rick Meyer
128 pages, 0-8066-4192-4

Rick Meyer contends that when children do not know they are deeply loved and cherished, persistent emotional deficits often result. The boys and men profiled in *I Love You, Son* reflect the struggles of adolescent boys and adult males as they face their own emotional deficits in relation to God, self, and others.

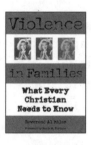

Violence in Families by Al Miles
176 pages, 0-8066-4264-5

Reverend Al Miles confronts the issues surrounding family violence its causes, and possible solutions. He also discusses how all people are affected and can help address the issue. This book provides guidance and information for lay people as well as for individuals experienced with the complex nature of domestic violence.

When Violence Is No Stranger by Kristin J. Leslie
200 pages, 0-8006-3575-2

Kristen Leslie offers the psychological and theological tools to religious professionals for understanding the deep spiritual trauma of the acquaintence rape survivor and how best to work with her to reconstruct a personal world of meaning, trust, and faith.

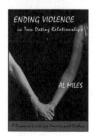

Ending Violence in Teen Dating Relationships by Al Miles
176 pages, 0-8066-5131-8

Miles, a nationally recognized expert in the field of domestic violence and teen relationship violence awareness, explores the complex issue of teen dating violence. Through interviews and other research, he provides critical information that parents, caregivers, clergy, and educators can use to protect teens and help them foster healthy dating relationships.

Available wherever books are sold.